Blessings of the Tanakh

Blessings of the Tanakh

Hebraica Veritas

Ken Bazyn

RESOURCE *Publications* · Eugene, Oregon

BLESSINGS OF THE TANAKH
Hebraica Veritas

Copyright © 2024 Ken Bazyn. All rights reserved. Except for brief quotations in critical publications or reviews, no part of this book may be reproduced in any manner without prior written permission from the publisher. Write: Permissions, Wipf and Stock Publishers, 199 W. 8th Ave., Suite 3, Eugene, OR 97401.

Resource Publications
An Imprint of Wipf and Stock Publishers
199 W. 8th Ave., Suite 3
Eugene, OR 97401

www.wipfandstock.com

PAPERBACK ISBN: 979-8-3852-1420-4
HARDCOVER ISBN: 979-8-3852-1421-1
EBOOK ISBN: 979-8-3852-1422-8

VERSION NUMBER 03/26/24

New Revised Standard Version, copyright 1989, Division of Christian Education of the National Council of Churches in the United States of America. Used by permission. All rights reserved.

Contents

Acknowledgments | vii
Introduction: Cain and Abel: Mystery of Evil | ix
Rachel: Missing Clay Gods | xix

Faith: | 2
An Addendum to Psalm 53 | 5
Hebrew *Hasid* | 8
If You Don't Do Good | 11
The Art of the Snare | 13
So You Wanna Go Back to Egypt | 15
One Metropolis Spared? | 18
Sodom's Hourglass | 20
In a Prophetic Tone | 23
Contrariwise | 26
The Selfish Gene | 29
Oh, for the Fleshpots of Egypt | 32
The Waterless Place | 34
The Faithless Shepherd | 37
Idolators | 39
Nonpareil: Who Can Be Compared to You? | 42
God Still Stands Indignant | 45
Here Come the Diminutive and Disfigured | 47
Golem | 50
Monarchist Pretensions | 52
Ahab to Elijah | 55
On Bonhoeffer's Participation in the Plot against Hitler | 58

To Tarshish I Fly | 60
A Ghoulish Gift | 62
Fractured Dreams | 64
SS Mutter | 67
Eden | 69
This Hermetically-Sealed Universe | 71
Am I Responsible? | 73
The Road Is Arduous | 76
Transitions | 79
The Wind Comes | 82
Geometric Figures in Whimsy | 84
Wet vs. Dry | 87
Tears: Nature's Safety Valve | 90
Exodus 28: Twelve Tribal Stones | 93
Notes from My Nervous Breakdown | 95
The Wart of God | 98
Wagging Manikin Faces | 101
Jacob's *Kuntz* | 104
A Little Yiddish Humor | 106
Joseph | 109
Yahweh vs. Horus | 111
You Have Become My Enemy | 113
In Anguish: God, You *Schlemiel* | 115
What! Is the Mocking Bird Here? | 118
What Does God Do? | 121
Inspired by Zechariah's Visions | 124
Messiah Coos and Mourns | 126
Ezekiel's Dry Bones | 129

Listing of Photographs | 131
Bibliography | 135

Acknowledgments

I WANT TO COMMEND Wipf & Stock for its ongoing commitment to publishing important books on a wide variety of topics from across the theological spectrum. In particular, I take my hat off to Calvin Jaffarian's excellent typesetting and layout as well as Rockbrook Camera in Omaha for conscientiously placing my 35 mm color slides onto a viable CD.

Too, my wife, Barbara, has labored with me long and hard to make the text as pleasing, accurate, and lyrical as possible. And Emily Callihan has faithfully questioned peculiarities of grammar, style, and content plus formatted the book with precision.

Credit is given here for the following poem:
"What! Is the Mocking Bird Here?" in *C.S.P. World News*

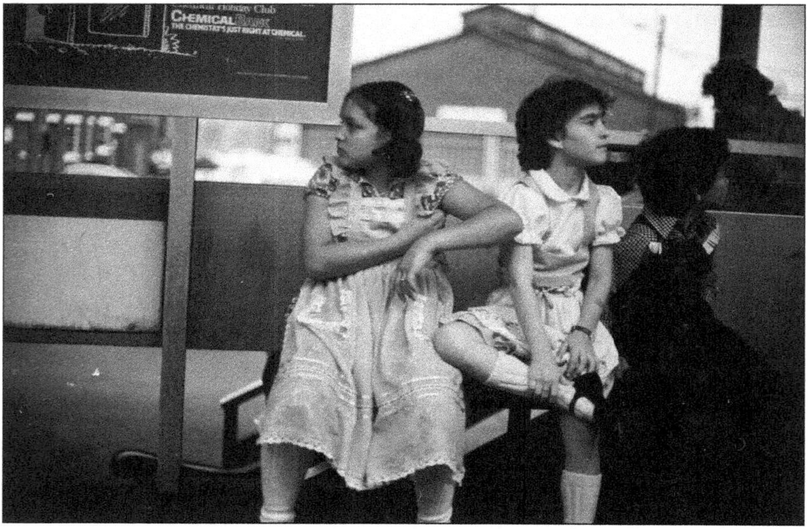
CHEMICAL
THE CHEMISTRY'S JUST RIGHT AT CHEMICAL

Introduction
Cain and Abel: Mystery of Evil

"Race of Cain, your agony,
Will it ever have an end?"

—Charles Baudelaire[1]

THE NARRATIVE OF CAIN AND ABEL is so typical of the book of Genesis. There are few concrete details, and powerful, unexpressed emotions play out against a virtually barren landscape.[2] Genesis deals with scenes of extraordinary psychological complexity—squabbles about everyday domestic life, questions of birthright, rivalry between brothers, acts of revenge, dreams sent from God, and so on. Cain is depicted there as both the first farmer and the first murderer. Because of the many unresolved questions in the story, commentators over the centuries have felt obliged to fill in the gaps. Here's the way key elements have been interpreted.

The first hint of tragedy comes in verses 4:4–5: "And the Lord had regard for Abel and his offering, but for Cain and his offering he had no regard." But why? One line of interpretation focuses on the offering itself. Abel had brought the firstborn of his flock, the fatty portions, while Cain had merely carried "an offering of the fruit of the ground" (v. 3). Later legends seized on this discrepancy, asserting that Abel sacrificed his finest lamb, while Cain just threw a few flax seeds on the altar.[3] For instance, in a medieval miracle play, Cain declares, "Here I tithe this unthende sheaf: /

---

1. "Abel et Cain" (my paraphrase), in Baudelaire, *Flowers of Evil*, 124.
2. Auerbach, *Mimesis*, 22–23.
3. Graves and Patai, *Hebrew Myths*, 91.

ix

Let God take it or else leave."[4] Another view is that the brothers were prompted by altogether different motives. Accordingly, Abel eagerly sought to please his creator, while Cain trudged along rather grudgingly. A third position claims that God preferred the blood of animals over vegetable offerings. (The book of Leviticus, however, indicates that both types are acceptable.)

God gives Cain time to mend his ways, but instead of bringing another, more worthy, offering, he becomes even more indignant, then slays his brother. (The close relationship between the two is emphasized seven times in this short narrative [vs. 2, 8–11] as Abel is called Cain's brother.[5]) When God's appears, however, Cain feigns ignorance, claiming, "I don't know what happened." How similar this is to the way Adam and Eve didn't want to admit that they had eaten of the forbidden tree in the garden (Gen 3:8–14). In his autobiography, C. S. Lewis as a reluctant convert to Christianity, spoke "of the steady, unrelenting approach of him whom I so earnestly desired not to meet."[6] Yet how can one hope to hide from an all-seeing God who is witness to all that we say or do? To make matters even worse, Cain flippantly adds, "Shall I shepherd the shepherd?" (translated as "Am I my brother's keeper?").[7] To what depths humanity has fallen from its time of innocence in the garden.

Ephrem of Syria describes the sequence of events this way: "God said to Cain, 'Why are you angry, and why is your face gloomy?' Instead of being filled with anger, you ought to be filled with distress. Instead of your face being gloomy, tears ought to be flowing from your eyes. 'If you do well, I will accept it.' . . . But instead of doing well so that the offering that had been rejected might be credited to Cain as acceptable, he then made an offering

---

4. "Cain and Abel" (N-Town cycle) in Cawley, *Everyman and Medieval Miracle Plays*, 30.
5. Sarna, *Understanding Genesis*, 30.
6. Lewis, *Surprised by Joy*, 182.
7. Rad, *Genesis*, 106.

of murder to that One to whom he had already made an offering of negligence."[8]

What precipitated this horrendous deed? The usual answer is envy. Cain saw Abel's sacrifice consumed and his rejected; then he directed his anger not at himself (hence repentance), but at his brother. Psychologists have gone on to speculate that there might have been an imbalance in family affection. Adam and Eve loved Abel, but were ill at ease with Cain. Thus the novelist John Steinbeck in *East of Eden* writes, "From his first memory Cal [Cain] had craved warmth and affection. . . . from the very first people were won instantly to Aron [Abel] by his beauty and his simplicity."[9]

Sin is crouching at Cain's door. As Dimitri, the oldest son in Dostoyevsky's *The Brothers Karamazov*, puts it, "There God and the devil are fighting for mastery, and the battlefield is the heart of man."[10] In *The Strange Case of Dr. Jekyll and Mr. Hyde*, Robert Louis Stevenson, too, depicts the divided self. Dr. Jekyll has discovered a drug that allows him to both change his appearance and his nature at will: "My devil had been long caged," but "he came out roaring. I was conscious, even when I took the draught, of a more unbridled, a more furious propensity to ill." Again: "The spirit of hell awoke in me and raged."[11] Mr. Hyde commits a senseless, sadistic murder, which shocks the respectable Dr. Jekyll, who expresses remorse.[12]

Sociologists, on the other hand, have seen the story more as a portrait of the rivalry between shepherds and grain farmers in early Mesopotamia than simply a tale of family jealousy. They point to such similar myths as the story of the two brothers Emesh and Enten in Sumeria. But in that story the air-god Enlil rewards the farmer, not the herdsman, and there the brothers are reconciled, as happens in later conflicts in Genesis between Esau and Jacob (Gen 32:6–8; 33:1–4) or Joseph and his eleven siblings (Gen 45:1–15).

---

8. Louth, *Genesis 1–11*, 105.
9. Steinbeck, *East of Eden*, 444.
10. Dostoyevsky, *Brothers Karamazov*, 124.
11. Stevenson, *Dr. Jekyll and Mr. Hyde*, 65.
12. Babbage, *Mark of Cain*, 31–34.

INTRODUCTION—*CAIN AND ABEL: MYSTERY OF EVIL*

>Emesh bent the knees before Enten,
>Into his house he brought . . . , the wine of the grape and the date,
>Emesh presents Enten with gold, silver, and lapis lazuli,
>*In* brotherhood and friendship, *happily*, they pour libations,
>Together *to act wisely and well they determined.*[13]

A few commentators, following S. H. Hooke, explain the murder as a ritual slaying. Cain was offering Abel to the field as part of a fertility rite. To do so, however, Hooke probably pays too much attention to v. 11: "The ground . . . has opened its mouth to receive your brother's blood."[14]

The punishment of Cain has caused much speculation. Many writers think that Cain was sentenced to be a nomad, wandering from place to place seasonally with his herds as opposed to the settled life of a farmer. If that's so, why is Cain also credited with building the first city (v. 17)? Anthropologists tend to see the punishment as a ritual taboo.[15] The murderer must be sent away lest he pollute others. In *The Golden Bough* James Frazer argues, "It is obvious that the blood of Cain's murdered brother is regarded as constituting a physical danger to the murderer; it taints the ground and prevents it from yielding its increase. Thus the murderer is thought to have poisoned the sources of life and thereby jeopardized the supply of food for himself, and perhaps for others."[16] An altogether different approach considers the punishment in terms of tribal law. So W. Robertson Smith observes, "A kindred group is a group within which there is no blood feud. If a man kills one of his own kin, he finds no one to take his part. Either he is put to death by his own people or becomes an outlaw and must take refuge in an alien group."[17] Cain certainly did become an outlaw and was cursed to wander.

---

13. "Emesh and Enten" in Kramer, *Sumerian Mythology*, 49–51.
14. Hooke, *Middle Eastern Mythology*, 124–26.
15. Radcliffe-Brown, "Taboo," 72–83.
16. Frazer, *Folklore in the Old Testament*, 34.
17. Smith, *Kinship and Marriage in Early Arabia*, 25.

INTRODUCTION—CAIN AND ABEL: MYSTERY OF EVIL

The mark Cain received, too, has been variously understood. Frazer thinks it possibly a disguise to prevent Abel's ghost from seeking revenge.[18] Others believe that it was a scar so repulsive that even those upset by Abel's death would show pity toward Cain. Some have regarded it as a simple tattoo that distinguished Cain from the rest of humankind. And a few have apparently confused Cain with the ancient Greek myth of Actaeon, for they believe when the elder brother was punished, he sprouted a horn from his head. It's important to notice God's mercy throughout. First, he gives Cain a chance to overcome his anger and make a second, more acceptable offering; then he encourages Cain to confess and own up to the murder; instead of executing him, God marks him for life, so that others will not kill him for doing away with his brother Abel.

The first homicide (and a fratricide at that!) may represent an important rite of passage. "Danger lies in transitional states," notes anthropologist Mary Douglas, "simply because transition is neither one state nor the next, it is undefinable. The person who must pass from one to another is himself in danger and emanates danger to others. The danger," she writes, "is controlled by ritual which precisely separates him from his old status, segregates him for a time and then publicly declares his entry to his new status."[19]

One finds a recurring motif of sibling competitiveness and jealousy throughout the Bible. Within Rebekah's womb two nations are struggling to be born (Gen 25:22–23). Jacob's sons sell the upstart Joseph to Midianite traders (Gen 37:25–28). In the Gospels, Jesus' half-brothers and sisters first opposed him, refusing to believe (John 7:3–10; Matt 13:55–56; Mark 6:3). In the parable of the prodigal son the elder brother objects to celebrating the younger one's return (Luke 15:11–32). Even Martha complains about her sister Mary's laziness to Jesus (Luke 10:38–42). "A brother offended is harder to win than a strong city," claims Prov 18:18 (NASB).[20]

18. Frazer, *Folklore in the Old Testament*, 41, 44.
19. Douglas, *Purity and Danger*, 96.
20. Ryken, et al., *Dictionary of Biblical Imagery*, 125–26.

INTRODUCTION—CAIN AND ABEL: MYSTERY OF EVIL

In his monumental *The City of God* (bk 15), Augustine expands this Cain-Abel struggle into a metaphor for the ongoing relationship between the city of man and the heavenly city.[21] It's interesting to note, too, how Luke (Luke 3:38), in tracing the lineage of Jesus, makes no mention of the branch of Cain, which has diverged from the main trunk, but refers instead to that next-born son of Adam and Eve, Seth, as the one who is the direct ancestor to the Messiah.

Echoes of Cain can be seen in the King Arthur cycle, in the stories of Balin and Balan,[22] of Modred, and of Launcelot, who kills his best friend, Gareth, and his sworn brother, Gawain. In *The Divine Comedy* Dante calls the lowest circle of hell Cocytus (*Inferno* 32);[23] there traitors to kin are punished by being buried up to their necks in ice, in a ring aptly named Caina.[24] In the Anglo-Saxon spirituality surrounding *Beowulf*, evil trolls, elves, and such monsters as Grendel and his mother are called Cain's descendants.[25]

To dramatize the story, I've written a short fictional monologue from Cain's rather jaundiced perspective. It is not meant to be taken literally but may help you to enter more fully into his feelings, ponder more deeply sin and the mystery of evil. You may disagree with some of my imaginative embellishments. We're not sure where to put Cain on the psychological spectrum, from the psychopath who knows no remorse, whom you might meet on death row in prison, to the obsessive-compulsive who is overly conscious of his guilt.

> My club is red, smeared with blood. My hand quivers and I am not yet thirty years of age. There lies my brother, Abel. His body is limp, his heart no longer pumps, his lungs are silent. A few minutes ago I was angry. Then we grappled. Now I am a ... a ... murderer!

---

21. Augustine, *City of God*, 595–648.
22. Malory, *King Arthur and His Knights*, 15–41.
23. Dean, "Cain," 121–22.
24. Gallagher, *To Hell and Back with Dante*, 6, 59.
25. Tuso, *Beowulf*, 3, 23, 200.

INTRODUCTION—CAIN AND ABEL: MYSTERY OF EVIL

(That was the first time I stammered, the first moment I ached for my companion.)

Memories of Abel are warm and near. When we were young, we made clay figures out of the mud, threw pebbles in a nearby stream, caught butterflies to present to Eve, our mother. Together we climbed trees, tamed a brown-and-white rabbit. Life was a dream and you never wanted to let go.

Yet somehow I felt apart from mother and father. When we ate, I often sat quietly, not knowing what to say, for fear that my words would reveal some hidden flaw. Out of doors I wanted to be left alone, so frequently I worked at the far end of the field. When we prayed, my feet wiggled and my hands played games almost involuntarily.

When I was seven, my father, Adam, told Eve, "Cain, our first-born, envies the attention we lavish on his younger brother." And Eve, wonderful Eve, replied, "He is still a boy. Soon he will grow out of this."

However, from that day on I never fully trusted my father. Yet perhaps he was right. Abel's spontaneity did overwhelm me. He was stronger than I. He could run faster. He knew how to shear sheep. He could even balance sticks on his toes longer than I. What parent isn't secretly prouder of their more successful son?

One day Abel called, "Let us offer a sacrifice to the Lord. He watches over us and grants us every good thing. He deserves our best." I agreed, and soon Abel was bringing his choicest lamb to the altar, while I grudgingly carried a few stalks of flax and bean seeds. It made a pitiful contrast, and God knew it. Yet Abel seemed more upset by God's rejection than I was. He said that God forgives more readily than father, but I doubted his words.

Afterwards we quarreled more and more. Once his sheep trampled my barley; I complained bitterly. Last year his sheep produced less manure than usual, so I blamed him for the poor harvest. And this year the rains came so late, if it hadn't been for mutton, our family might have gone hungry. I despised his blasted luck. So I demanded

INTRODUCTION—*CAIN AND ABEL: MYSTERY OF EVIL*

that he pasture his sheep far from my planted ground. When he would not, I rose up and slew him.

Why does the earth not swallow up my brother's cries as it does the last bleatings of the slaughtered sheep? And why is the spite in my chest not now relieved? Instead, it seems to have forged an altogether new channel and weighs on me even more heavily. And why does God seek me when I mean not to be found?

He already rejected the sacrifice of me, the eldest, the firstborn, who should have been most worthy of his favor. Will he punish me as he did father and mother, who were banished from paradise, condemned to years of suffering and pain, who had to hoe thorns and thistles in a lifetime of back-breaking labor? He is a cruel and arbitrary deity. I want nothing to do with him. Torment me, God, tattoo me, turn me again into dust, but I'll have none of your mercy.

Yet I fear for my life. The whole world seems eager to cut it short. Even the beasts of the field are anxious to devour me. I hear the mountains and valleys ring out, "Fratricide! Fratricide!" My parents consider me a vagabond, unfit for their sight. And undisturbed sleep is far from me.

Eyes, where are your tears? Mouth, where are your words of repentance? Knees, where is your earnest supplication? When I put my hoe in the earth to cut off a noxious weed, overnight it springs up again. I dig holes, plant my seeds, then wait for the nurturing rains, only to watch in horror as the withered stems are washed away by downpours.

Adam called me over: "Son, you must flee far from this place. God will give you a mark for your protection, so even the desperate will show you compassion. Here, take your sister to be your bride. Cover the earth with descendants, and pray to God that your children will not have so angry a brow."

Therefore, Cain left the only relatives he ever knew and traveled to Nod, a land of nightmares and sorrow, where even the whippoorwill refused to sing. There he built a fortress and found his anonymity. From his union came forth the seeds of civilization:

music, metallurgy, architecture, government. We, his children, as German philosopher Jakob Boehme declares, "no longer walk together in the love of God; but, full of passion, we envy, vilify, dishonor, and denounce one another, wishing to one another death and all kinds of evil."[26] This is the legacy of Cain—and of Adam. The only one who is really happy, poet Christina Rossetti writes, is "the serpent in the dust / Wriggling and crawling, / [who] Grinned an evil grin, and thrust / His tongue out with its fork."[27]

Let us pray.

> We know deep in our heart of hearts that Cain is our forebear as well as Abel. We have within us both the propensity to do good and seething passions anxious to break forth into evil. Give us the self-control that we so desperately need to transmute devilish inclinations into God-honoring deeds, lest the sin crouching at our door overpower us and drag us near to the abyss. When we quarrel, show us the way of reconciliation, provide for us a mediator. Amen.

---

26. Whyte, *Bible Characters*, 31–32.
27. "Eve," in Atwan and Wieder, *Chapters into Verse*, 48.

Rachel: Missing Clay Gods

"WHY DID YOU TAKE THOSE IDOLS?" Jacob asked me. Not once, twice, but more like a hundred times I've heard those words since we left my father Laban's house. And Jacob says it in such an accusing tone, as though I were somehow blaspheming against the god of Abraham and the fear of Isaac.

Jacob is too harsh. I've heard that our neighbors—the Amorites, the Babylonians, the Egyptians, the Minoans—all construct visual images of their gods. An idol maker is a most respected craftsman. He chooses the finest metals—gold, silver, copper—the most durable stone—marble, limestone, granite—and the most beautiful wood—cedar, cypress, acacia—to make likenesses. His large statues adorn temples; his small ones guard the households. (Of course, some of these craftsmen are also shrewd businessmen and deliberately make ambiguous figures, which can be sold in several different markets at once.)

I think these idols are among the greatest art treasures of our day. Consider the beautiful pyramids of Egypt, which represent the sacred stone of Re; the ziggurats of Mesopotamia, which symbolize the nearness of god to man; and the sacred bulls of Amurru, which stand for the warrior-god Baal. Some are rather scary, though, such as those bulging eyes of Abu, the pronounced breasts of Astarte, and the dreaded jaws of that monster Aman.

But Jacob doesn't agree. He claims that the God of Abraham is jealous. Since he created the heavens and earth, how can we worship him with handcrafted images? He cannot be likened to animals, plants, stars, rocks, or human beings. This detracts from his majesty, and some people may believe that the idol is a god, not just a symbol.

Yet I wonder: Should we abandon the ways of our forefathers to serve some mysterious, all-embracing being? I feel more secure worshipping familiar gods who have proven themselves worthy over the years. The hill country can be a hostile place. You need kinsmen more than you need a new god.

Gods are not always trustworthy. Sometimes they seem remote, unwilling to help in time of need. Sometimes they are defeated in battle by neighboring gods, so you begin to doubt their powers. Sometimes they fall down and break; then new ones must be purchased or constructed quickly. Otherwise, bad luck is sure to come. But Jacob's God has prospered him time and time again, despite the wiles of my unscrupulous father. Jacob is certainly true to his name; first he supplanted his brother's birthright and now he has my father's livestock.

Maybe Jacob is right. Some gods can represent the depraved imagining of sick souls, not the noblest longings of the human mind. Certainly, tales of jealousy, adultery, arrogance, and torture don't encourage good behavior.

But let's be practical for a moment. I stole the gods so Jacob could inherit from my father. Now, even if Laban does give birth to additional sons, our rights can never be taken away. That's why he chased us, not because of his "piety." In fact, Laban was forced to make a new covenant with Jacob when he couldn't find the gods. (Shh—I had actually been sitting on them in my saddle bag.) Otherwise, his own sons would have been in jeopardy.

But Jacob is stubborn. When he found out I had stolen the family idols, he reprimanded me severely—partly to save face, since he had acted so cavalierly before my father, and partly because he is so religious. Jacob's God even reveals himself through dreams. Then Jacob will hallow the place by erecting a stone pillar and pouring out a libation. (He doesn't call these idols, but memorial stones.) His God is interested in our everyday affairs, in fair play, and shuns the magical formulas of so many other deities. He calls for the circumcision of all covenant males. And he allegedly controls human destiny, the weather, and fertility.

RACHEL: MISSING CLAY GODS

How can these things be? No one, except possibly a king, is so gifted that he can govern so many realms at once. It makes more sense to have one god in charge of the sky, one in charge of the earth, and one ruling over the subterranean world, and so on. The God of Abraham promises a little too much. And what if he can't deliver?

I guess I'm rather traditional. Preserve the past, carefully glean from what's new. Giant steps are just too frightening. Maybe someday I'll change my mind and completely follow in my husband's footsteps. But for the time being I'm content to keep these idols around where Jacob can't find them. After all, when emergencies come, there's no harm in praying to every conceivable god who might be able to help you.

1

Faith:

"To beleeve onely possibilities, is not faith, but meere Philosophy."[1]
—Thomas Browne

A strand thrown out by the spider's spinneret,
a thread of expectations lassoed to a sacred vault,
a rope to pull together two mighty continents,
a casting line that lands the gefilte fish.

The cable that emboldens us to swing
across the canyons of finitude,
the taut chain dragging us out of inadvertent potholes,
the guy that generates assurance of salvation,
the cord as long as the comet's tail and as short as a widget.

The plumb line that measures how firm our resolve,
the tightrope to walk between
the clashing rocks of doubt and temptation,
the diamond link of plighted troth,
the retrieving arrow that joins the marksman to his quarry,
the tether safely anchored we're forever testing,

---

1. Endicott, ed., *Prose of Sir Thomas Browne*, 55.

The olive branch conveying nutrients from Eden,
the omni-directional antenna that tunes our self-perception,
the elastic bond which gives at both ends,
the circuit that shocks us into *caritas*,
the wind-tossed fiber which breaks   should we let go.

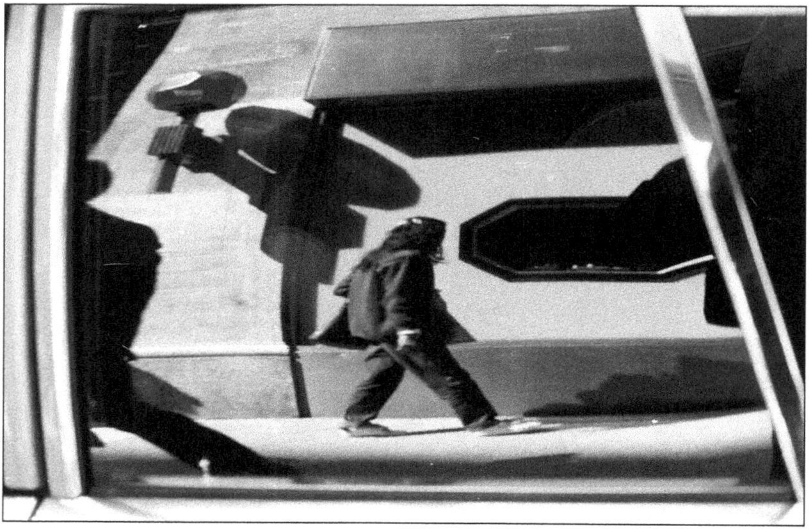

An Addendum to Psalm 53

As it is written, None is righteous,
  No, not one,
  None seek after God, all flee from his face!
All are sick unto death,
All bereft of prenatal innocence,
All spite their neighbor,
All resent the unequal distribution of wealth,
All revile God like malevolent Haman:
  Flesh jousting with Spirit,
  Law slaying Conscience,
  Reason at odds with the Act,
  Pride inlaid with Aggression,
  Lust filling out simple Desire.

When I want to do good,
evil sprouts in my heart,
if sacrifice and kindness come to my head,
paternalism and so what? squelch my hands,
  Michael and Lucifer twins,
  monozygotic Jachin and Boaz,
  to the world a luminous halo,
  before those in the know a conniving Adrammelech.

The Holy One (blessed be he)
gives Everyman his say,
fast-talking lawyers perspire before omniscient robes,
    will *Selbsterkenntnis* occur
    along this corridor of mirrors?
    the ghost occupy its haunted bone house?
    the heart prove heavier than the feather of Ma'at,
    or shall the blood o'er the doorposts speak?

    II

If the whole is relative,
no definite beginning or clear end,
how then is heaven conceived?
and if the soul seeps out the head,
does it exist independent or not,
is it neither or both?
a few sadly shake their heads and hope.

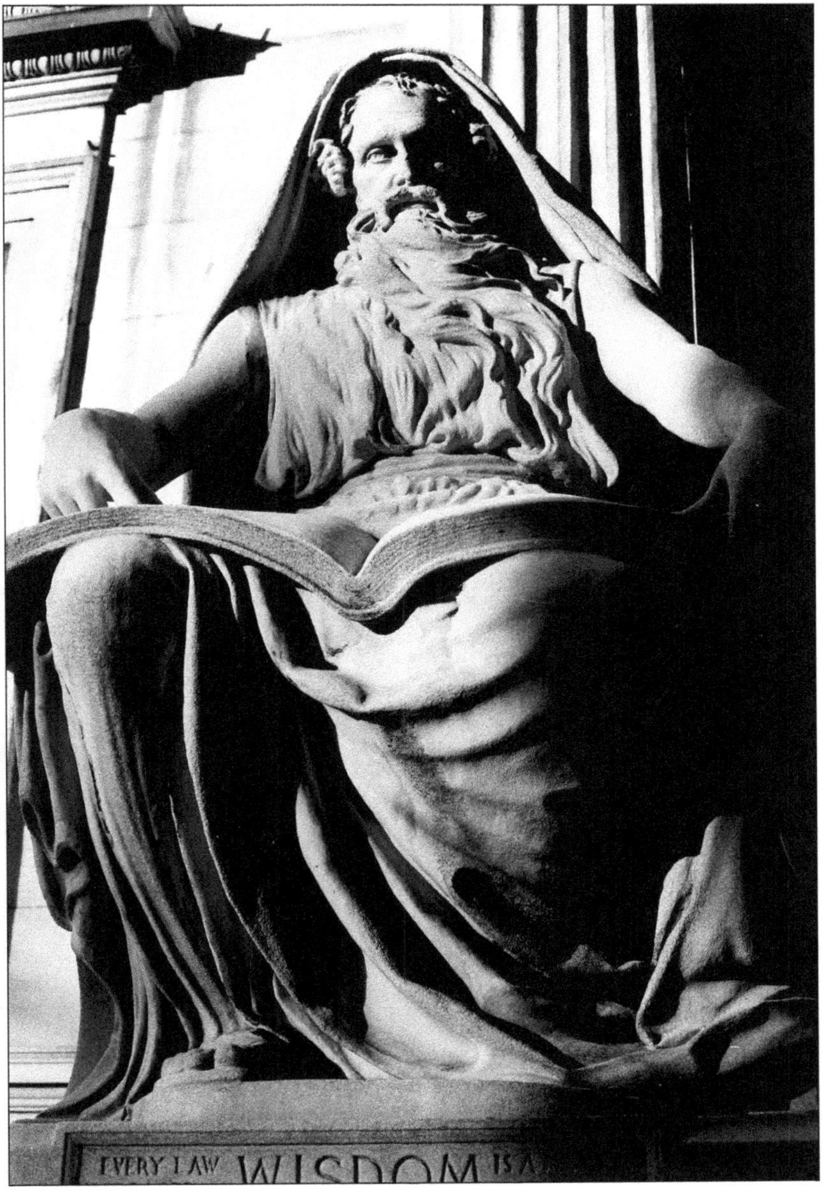
EVERY LAW
WISDOM

Hebrew *Hasid*

Moses committed murder,
the eleven patriarchs sold the twelfth as a slave,
Abraham sought to palm off his wife as his sister,
Saul hurled spears at his concert lyre,
David had Uriah pinned against a siegework wall,
then quickie-married that knockout Bathsheba,
even Hezekiah grew injudicious with age.

Jacob duped his ailing father,
Solomon was enticed by foreign, shimmying wives,
Sarah couldn't believe in her own post-menopausal fertility,
Samson scorched the Philistines with burning flax and
    uproarious riddles,
Jonah boarded a ship heading for the antipodes,
then pouted beneath an umbrella plant, which wilted,
    once Nineveh had repented,
out of the fire, master goldsmith Aaron molded a blasphemous calf.

Which Israelite monarch ever removed all of the high places
or tore down the Asherim?
at first Esther wavered in her support for Mordecai, then relented,
Gideon put out his fleece—twice,
Jeremiah was so despised he became suicidal,
Noah fell to drinking once the waters had subsided,
it took two angels to arm-twist and rescue Lot.

How many of that miracle-weary band ever set foot
   on promised soil,
how many rather were bitten by serpents, given over to plagues,
died of an inordinate craving?
of the twelve original tribes only one remained true
and what portion of that?
Hebrew hagiography then consists of moments
of profound Abrahamic faith, reluctant acts of obedience—
against a backdrop of stiff-necked, protracted self-assertion,
not unlike what any scrupulous account of the church's
   seesaw behavior would also reveal.

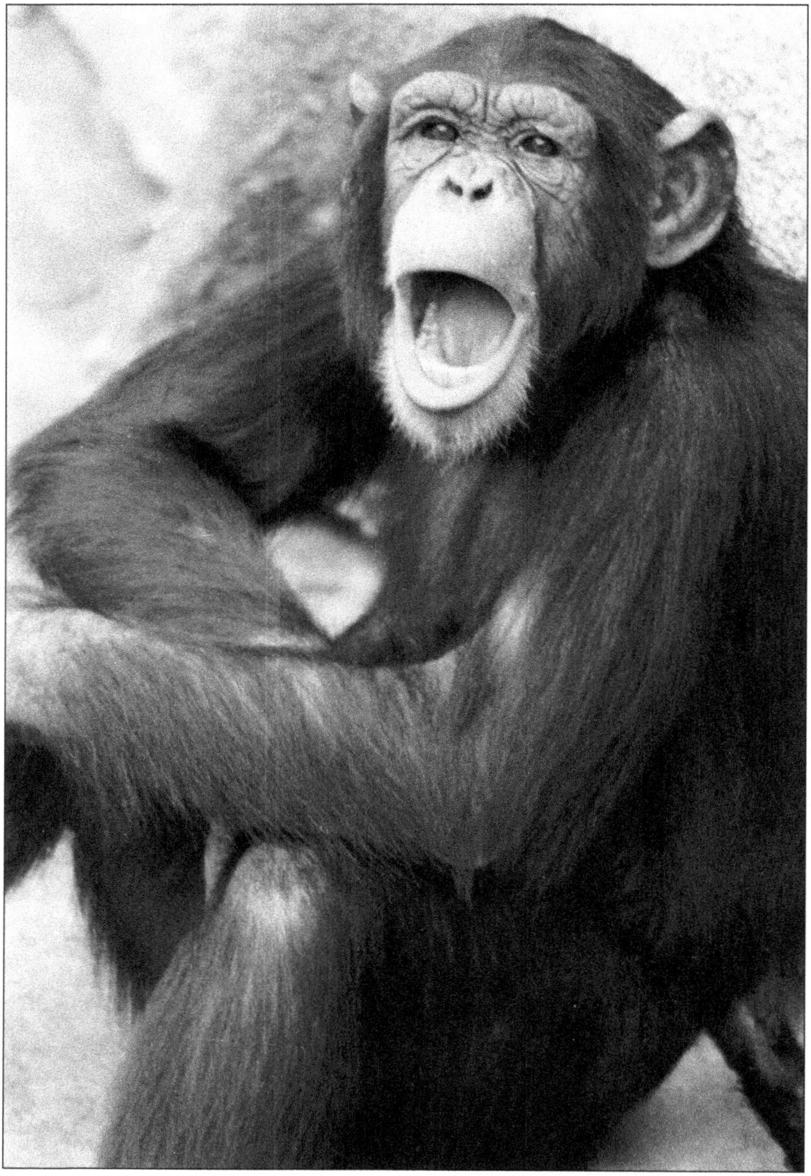

If You Don't Do Good

It almost never hurts if you don't do good,
it just sits there nonchalantly.

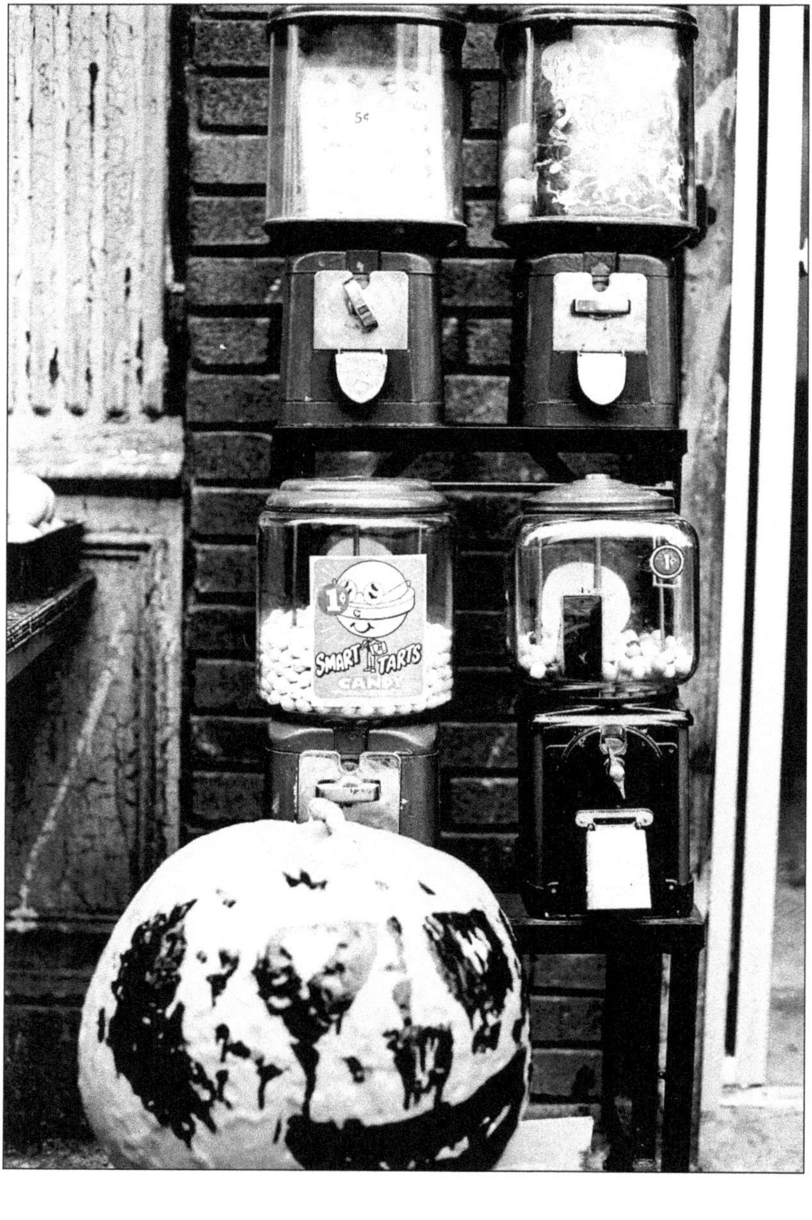
5¢
1¢
SMART TARTS
CANDY
1¢

The Art of the Snare

Fools can be flattered,
just roll out an easy chair to entrap the self-indulgent,
bake bonbons for the glutton.

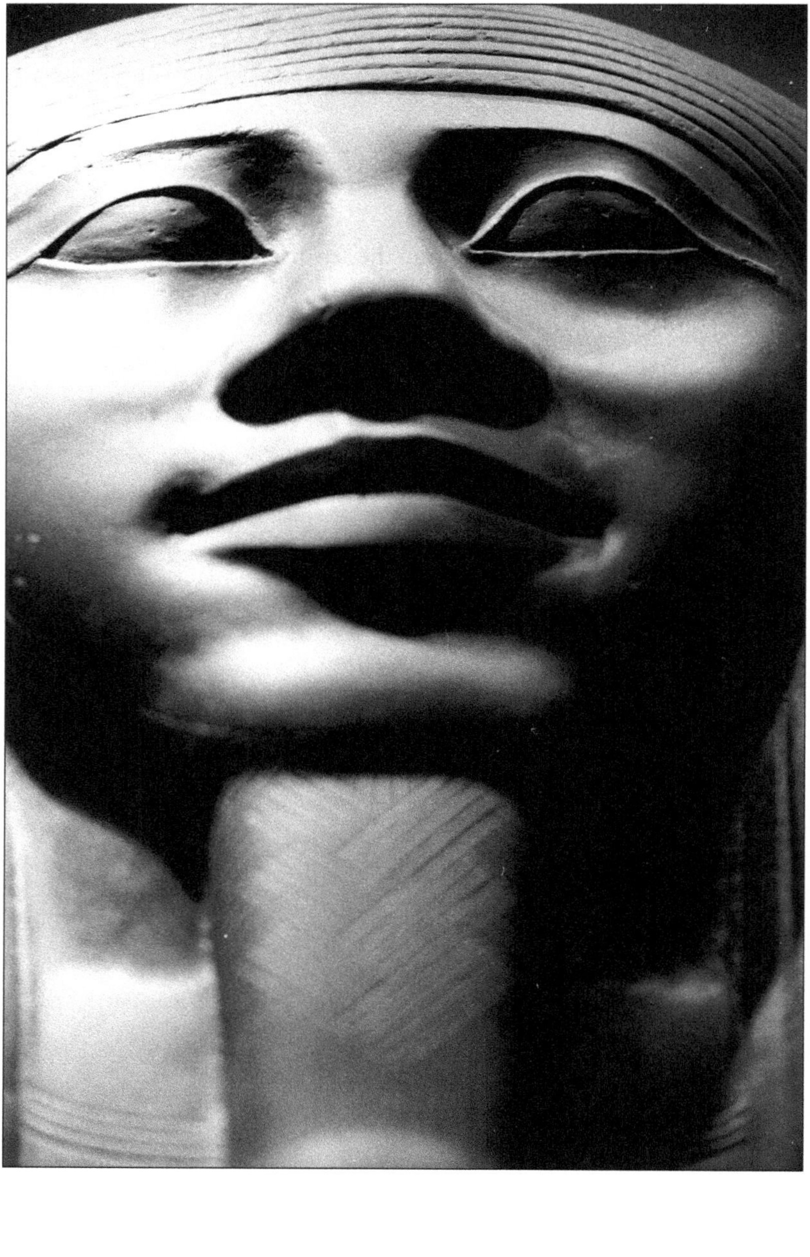

So You Wanna Go Back to Egypt

So you wanna go back to Egypt
where cucumbers, melons, onions,
leeks, and garlic grew,
bouquets of bluebells, water lilies,
and the Folies-Bergère,
sun-worshipping crocodiles,
animal-headed goddesses,
a crowded pantheon, but no Magna Carta.

We have eaten of the tree of knowledge
and its fruit is ghastly green:
soma outranking fortitude,
lucre a notch *über* honesty,
the unleavened matzo bread
less delectable than Memphis porridge,
a white plumed crown and curly ostrich feathers
more reliable than flaky wafers resembling hoarfrost.

In the garden of the gods
Pharaohs were immortal,
the mirror, sword and jewel
could put the Hyksos and the Hittites on the run,
Moses's bronze serpent
vs. Isis and faithful Horus,
a smoking Matterhorn and molten calf,
though Re triumphs each morning.

Moses sucking his bulrush thumb
where a blooming Hebrew boy left his cloak,
tomorrow lay at the bottom of a diviner's cup,
The Book of the Dead had 42 amulet locks to pick
and a court as refined as a Noh play.
For our mother Nile and sister wheat—
we'd swap 40 years of pestilence,
a pillar of cloud and an intermittent fire.

Who is the sternest taskmaster:
Horeb Yahweh or Theban Pharaoh?

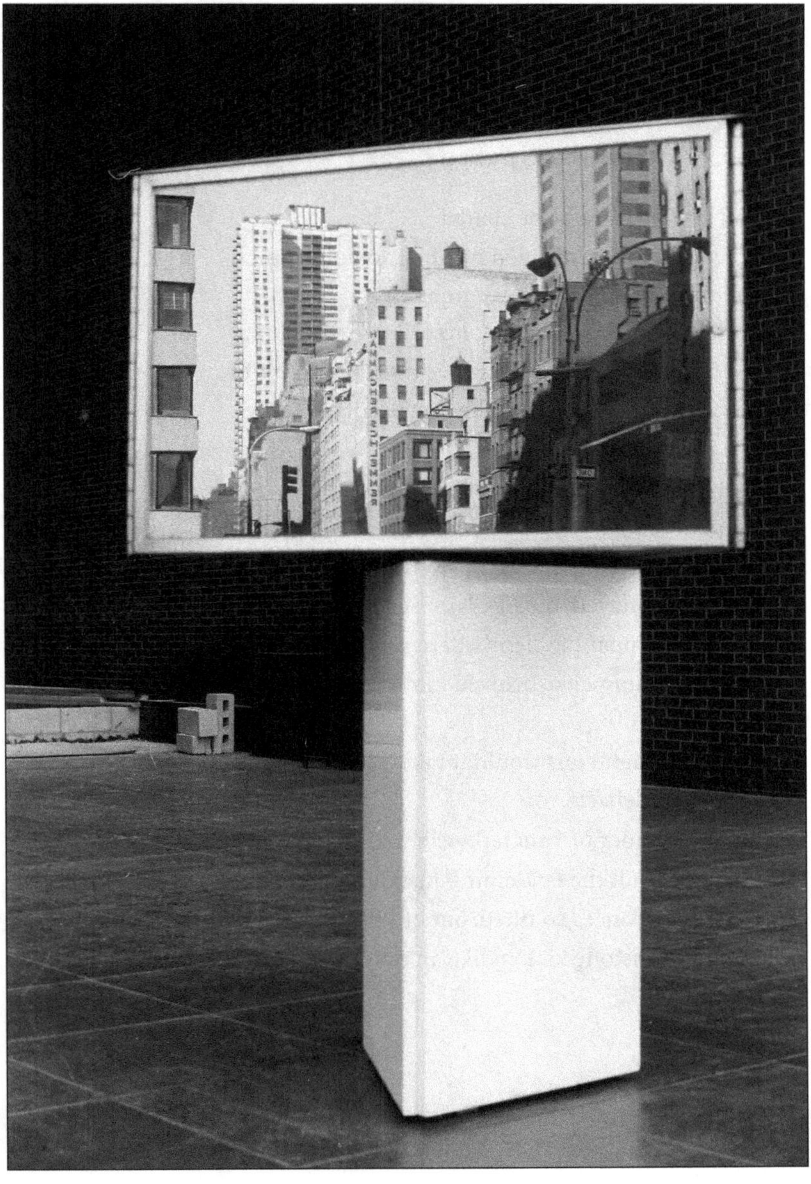

One Metropolis Spared?

Shall one metropolis be spared
and another be consumed by blue, noxious fumes,
shall one polis contract gangrene
and its twin undergo green, luxuriant expansion,
how can one tell if his collective bowl of iniquities
is overbrimming, about to be poured out?

Justice is as elusive as a zigzagging bull's eye,
the highest offices are bought and sold like gunny sacks of barley,
a deep cleavage separates those cultivated from the *ebyon* or peon,
children are flayed, the headstrong loosed,
disease is rampant in dens where sex is swapped for inebriation,
mules are pummeled, bruised into goose-stepping submission.

How many righteous would it take
to stave off debacle,
if say, X number of *ba'al teshuvah* went to yeshivah,
would that halt the epidemic—just outside our gates,
or are the balances so tilted, out of kilter,
fire and brimstone kick in like an overripe machete?

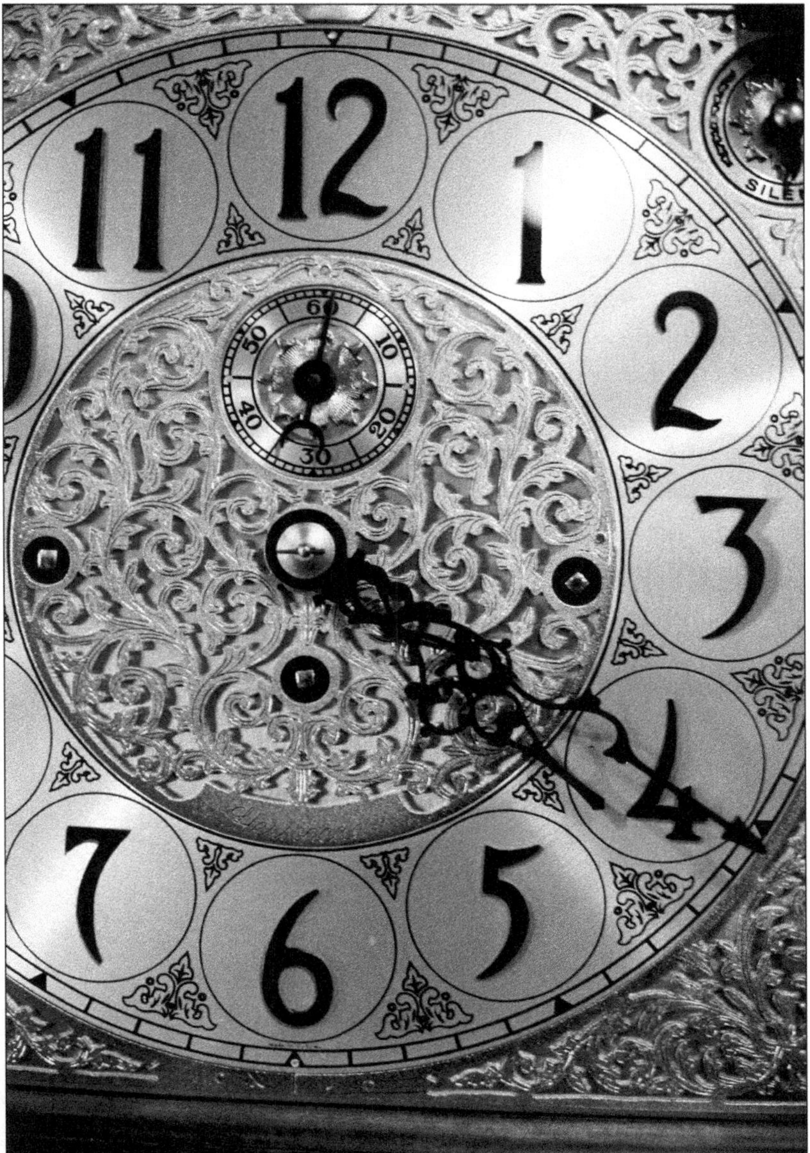

Sodom's Hourglass

Sand drips inexorably
through the Victorian-corseted waist,
time like an abrasive shower
lodges in hair, shirt, and throat,
nothing can plug that Pandoran leak.

The transparent Venetian skin
bubbles and squeezes
into funnel-shaped dirges,
while alto trombones fortissimo
our pitiable demise.

Clock springs must be wound taut,
hourglasses turned invariably by hand,
for no rotating Swiss folk dancers
or redwood comic cuckoos
can possibly relieve that mechanical tedium.

There is just the annoying drip-drip from a desert faucet,
white lost in saguaro white
like some rote Negev ritual
which measures smaller and less divisible fractions
of a commodity nearly precipitate.

Beads of foolishness and grains of courage
slip through the gravity flow sieve,
are buried, lost in amorphous drifting dunes
which historians sift, continuously readjust,
alert for any debris left by Lot's wife and her forebears.

Nun, gimmel, hay, and *shin.*

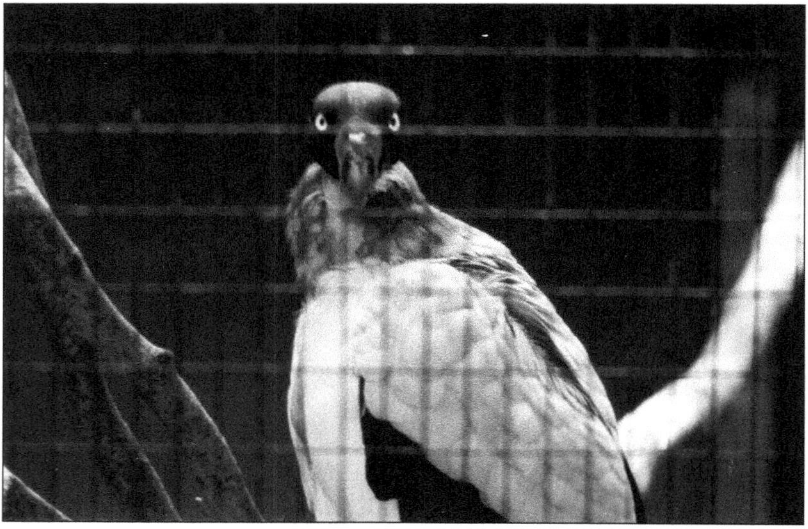

In a Prophetic Tone

I unseat despots,
confuse counselors,
create widespread panic
among invading forces.
Stubborn, indolent peoples
I blot out
with gum eraser strokes.

I stop the mouths
of chronic liars, cheats,
avenge the slain
with boomerang-swift rapiers.
When nations exceed
their allotted bounds,
I stand back,
withdraw my shielding fingers.

The lowly I lift
on white, gorgeous steeds,
disperse throughout my fabled realm.
The prosperous I urge
to dig deeper
into their bulging, padlocked pockets.

Floral trophies, crowns—I hurl—
as well as withered laurel medallions
into the forge of my bitter rage.
To the foolish
I call out with brazen, intrepid shouts:
    Turn back
from your corkscrew descent.

The selfless shall see
my gentle, beleaguered, features
shrouded by a numinous cloud;
the truly terrified, moreover,
will behold my righteous, incandescent center.

   Ein Keloheinu!

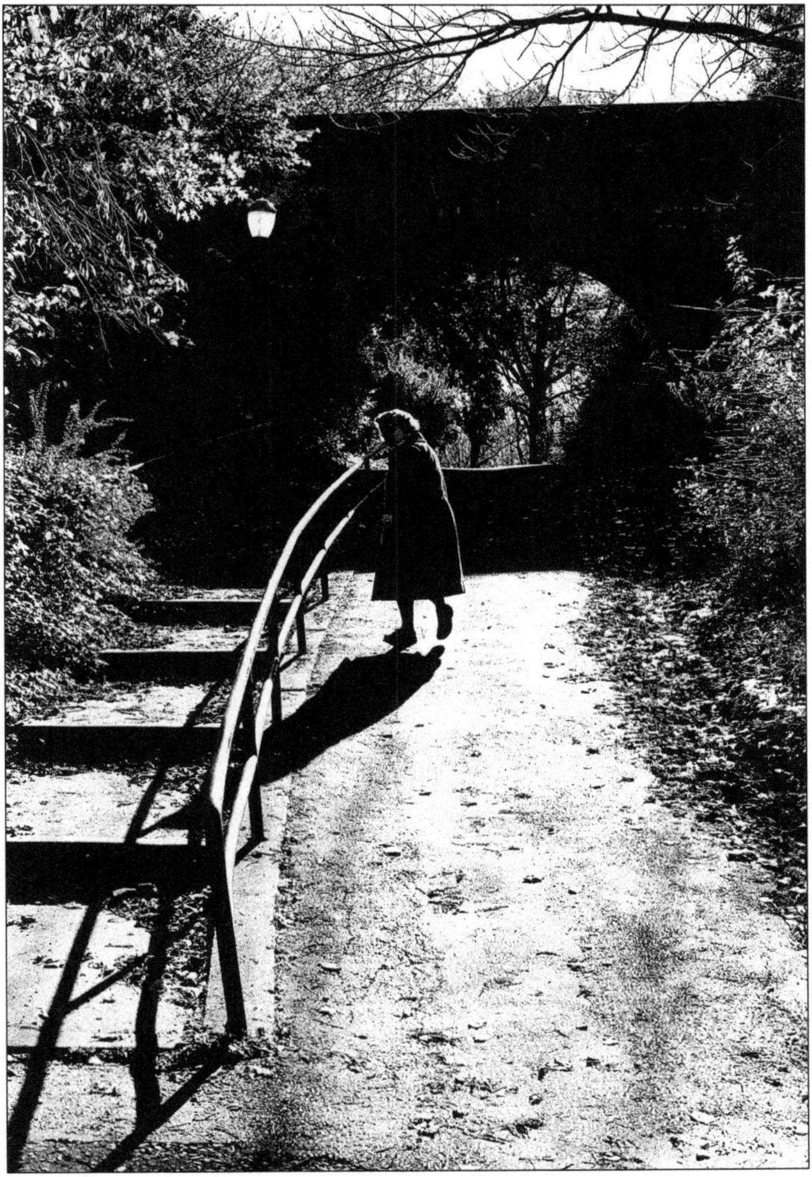

Contrariwise

I will walk contrary to you
if you despise and affront me,
turn aside from revealed paths
to wallow in suffocating deceit.

I will give you over to vain imaginings
should you dishonor me with your vile passions,
if you flagrantly provoke, transgress, and rebel—
crush or grind innocent Abel's skull.

I will take off my gentleman gloves,
let loose that pulverizer the Lying Deceiver, the Lawless One,
if you persist in betraying strangers and aliens,
allow the orphan and widow to grow emaciated.

I will tear up these two tablets of stone with my bare hands
should you finger gold and silver figurines,
bow down before likenesses of cloven-footed behemoths
    or flying reptiles,
fail to express gratitude to your all-beneficent Creator.

My soul will abhor you and your children's children,
and I will remove my abode from your midst,
if you heed the voice of demented demons
and sacrifice even one living infant.

I will turn my back upon and disown you,
regard you as bastards, siblings of stone,
if you reject my benign ordinances and statutes,
I will pretend *you* never existed.

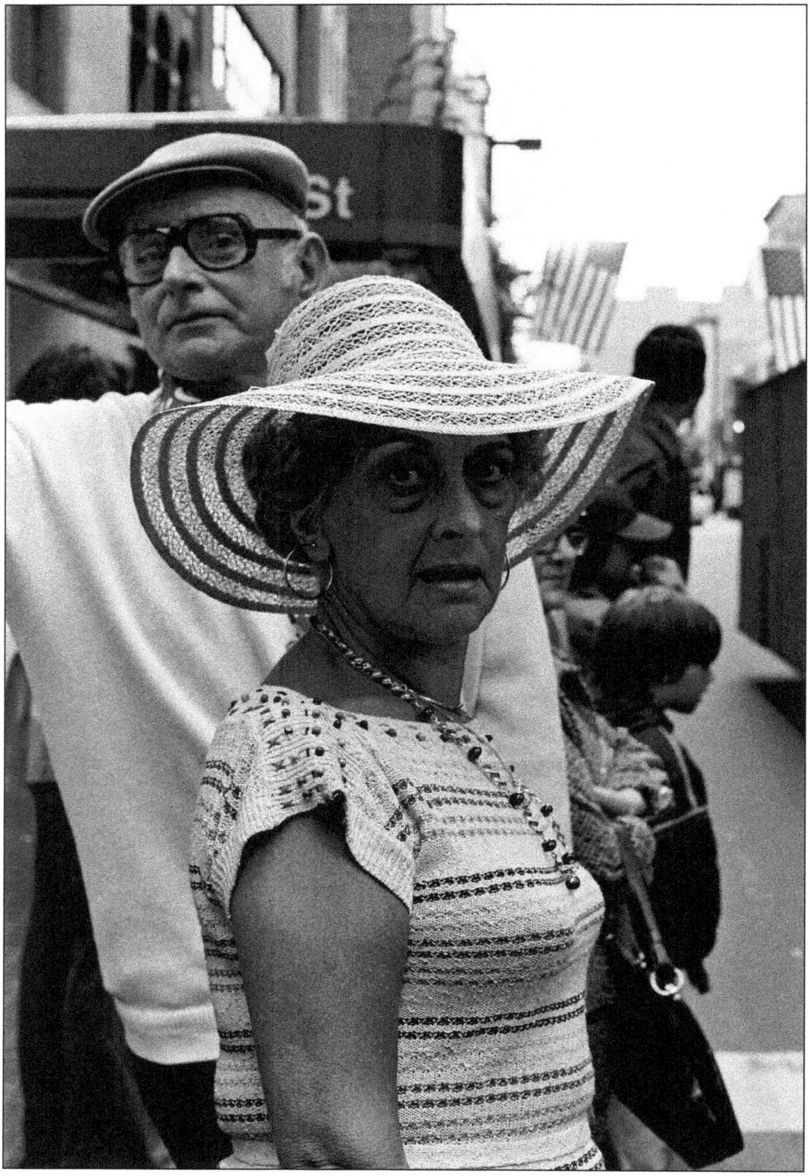

The Selfish Gene

O Lord, rend the heavens
and shoot thy Savior down,
the nations mock divine decrees,
with insolence they bind
the free man in usurious chains,
make the drunkard captive of his cup,
artificially pump the brain dead's involuntary valves,
rescue the fetus, while all about
malnourished children and adults
hang threadbare from multinational corporate trees.

Let the educated, the bright, the well-endowed
scoop out places more impressive than they deserve,
assuming the good yeast will rise into a loaf,
the bad will neither flourish nor disdain.

O Lord, the selfish gene thus defends
itself with cerebral, verbal cunning,
grand sweeps of generalization,
statistics (pick and choose),
surrounds itself with a moat and wall,
laying bricks of inherent superiority and caste.

Aristocratic pretensions—I despise—
no man has a right to crush his fellow,
though gross inequality expand unabated,
we must at all times and everywhere
fight its *raison d'être*.

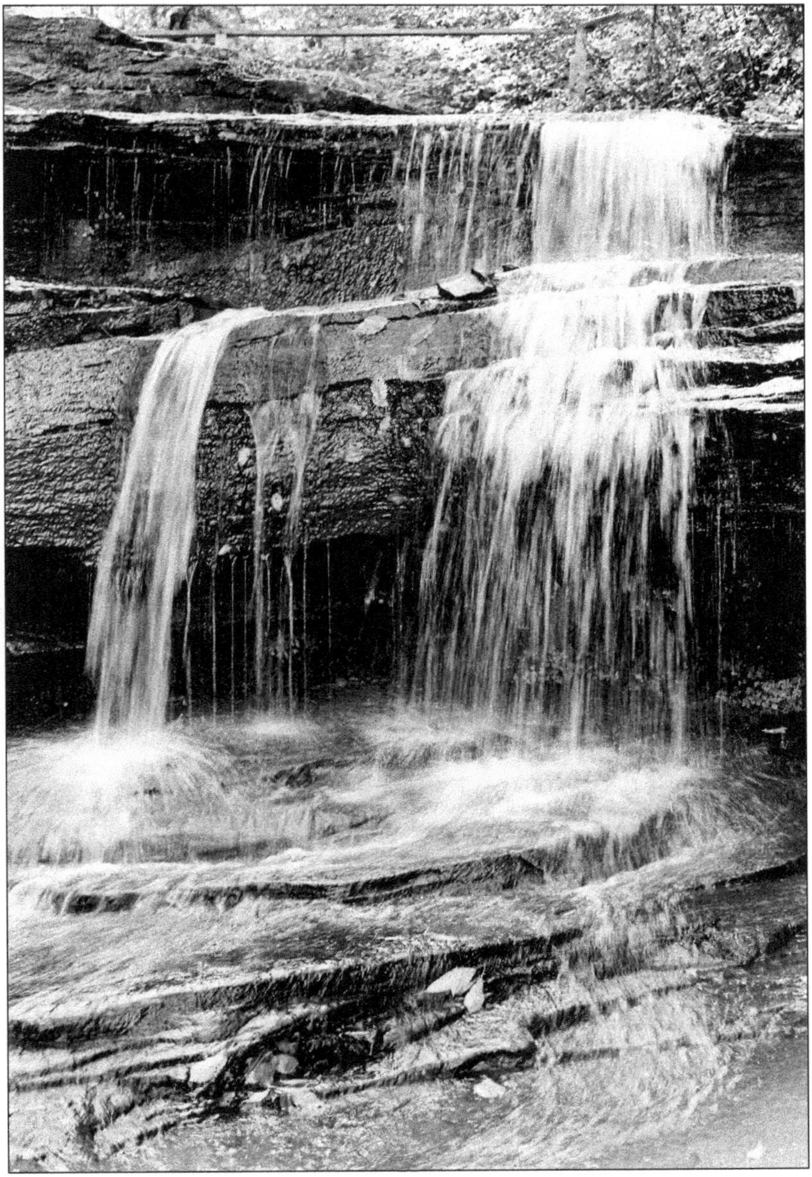

Oh, for the Fleshpots of Egypt

God prepared for them a banquet in the wilderness,
set out the bread of angels on platters,
rained down gusts of quail in intemperate squalls,
made water flow from flint rock.

Yet still they spurned his prevenient pleading,
yearned for fish, leeks and garlic—the fleshpots of Egypt—
believing those sun-dried brick/ball-and-chain taskmasters
less fearsome than a first-born destroyer.

Rescued from lives as Semitic chattel, they despoiled the Egyptians,
scampered across a Red Sea carpet,
chariot wheels clogging and churning in the mud,
while mammoth waves came crashing down.

Pyramids are heady, man-god stuff,
though the chosen people's future lay rather in the run-off
    from glacial hills,
of course, giants would still need to be outwitted, catapults set up
    against fortified walls,
tribal unity coalesce. . . . but, for the moment, each reminisced
    of rustic Nile huts.

Ah! how the past is Poussin/pastoral/romantic,
the future, foreboding Hieronymous Bosch/surreal/fantastic.

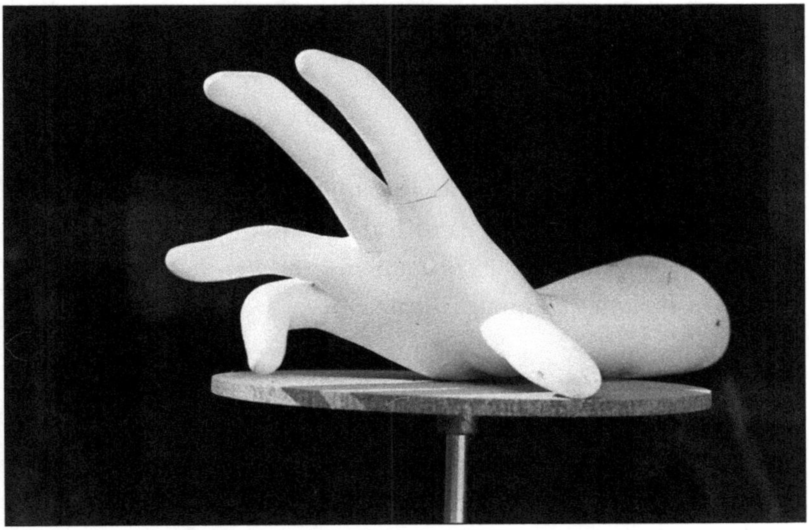

The Waterless Place

Moses heard a voice,
but he saw no zoomorphic image,
God stenciled his demands on notebooks of stone,
yet his stylus was a disembodied finger,
he was known by no occult name, had no consort,
nor did he entertain fertility or enthronement rites,
when he spoke it was through a veil.

If the mountains shuddered,
a plague coursed through the camp,
manna fell from a calm and cloudless sky,
idolators or rebels were overcome by cruel or unusual deaths,
still his holiness was guarded by the sons of Aaron's
    consecrated hands,
which first had to atone for their own misgivings
before offering up communal, unblemished rams.

Murmurers might be cut off,
those of the inordinate craving
cut down by their belly's greed,
Moses's spirit be apportioned to seventy faithful men,
while God's intentions were revealed via a peripatetic column
    of smoke or water vapor,
nevertheless, his intractable people so often put him to the test,
his grievances became legend.

He would have his people struggle, wend
their way through an uncharted wilderness,
triumph over all manner of prickly obstacles
to reach that waterless place,
and there to acknowledge him as their true tutelary genius,
who pours out savory, unabated refreshment,
the only Deliverer who will never, no never, do them
   irreparable harm.

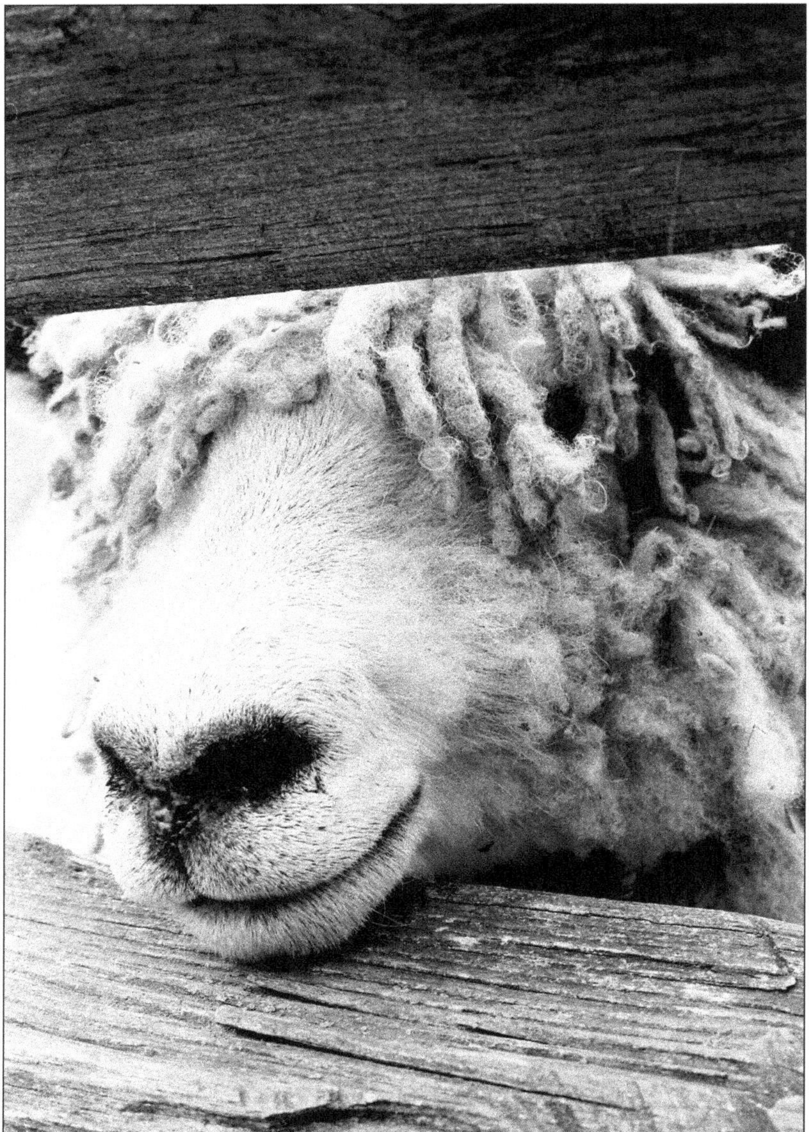

The Faithless Shepherd

I am the faithless shepherd
who pastures the sheep beside poisonous streams,
terrorizes the flock with hired wolf calls,
staves off the crippled when his own lifeboat is threatened,
lets the strays wander off to their own precipitous doom.

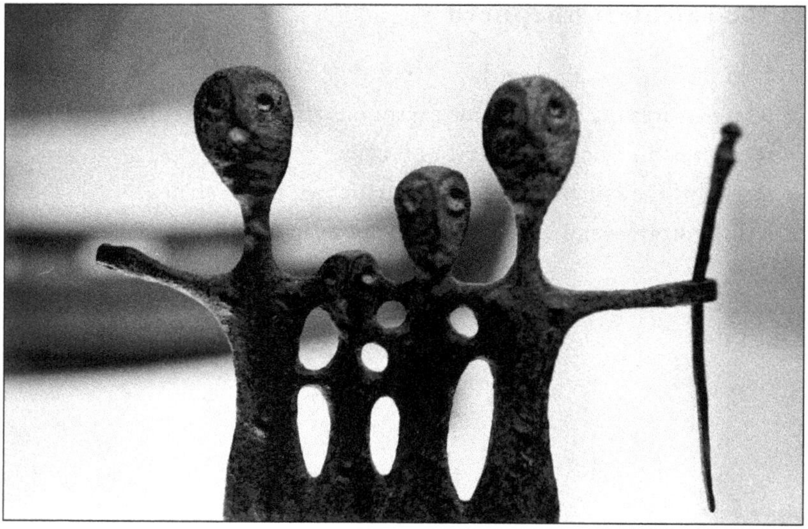

Idolators

My beloved brethren,
once you galloped proud as zebras,
now you crawl like slithering cobras,
your message of joy and release to the captives
has been stifled and thwarted by ungodly tyrants,
not a few of which have succumbed to the darts and wiles of
   the Evil One,
denying the Lord whom they covenanted with on
   the belching mountain,
of these Enoch prophesied:
men will walk in the way of Ahab,
following abominable painted idols,
casting out Jacob's descendants as carrion for peccaries,
mighty *Nephilim* who would revile the glorious angels
if their mouths were not abruptly stopped.

I have watched many such pretenders
ogle for authority, prance for position,
swear by the name of occult figurines,
theirs is the way Cain trod envying righteous Abel,
their half-burnt sacrifices and moldy cereal offerings
rise up as a stench in Elohim's nose,
they are like uprooted oaks,
waves whose main force has been spent far offshore,
disorderly malcontents, grumblers
who worship their own expanding gut,

hypocrites whose svelte skin and silken garments
betray a charnel house of cinder,
their fall is Belshazzar sure.

THE SEARCH FOR
ALEXANDER THE GREAT
HE SEARCHED
FOR IMMORTALITY.
SOME BELIEVED
HE SUCCEEDED.
AN EXTRAORDINARY
4-PART
TELEVISION DRAMA
BEGINS MAY 6
WEDNESDAYS
10 PM CHANNEL 13 PBS
HOST: JAMES MASON
MADE POSSIBLE
BY A GRANT
FROM MOBIL
SUBWAY

Nonpareil: Who Can Be Compared to You?

Who can be compared to you, O matchless one,
where is your peer or equal?
who knows the end from its beginning,
speaks and it's a fait accompli?
who beckons the winds as messengers,
flames of fire, slaves?
    Dayenu.

Seated high above fallible mortals
in a dense, impenetrable cloud,
surrounded by compliant seraphim and cherubim,
you rule galaxies with a thumb,
before you cordillera rumble, stars quaver,
life-forms fret, do obeisance, turn contrite.
    Dayenu.

Your purposes are beyond all earthly ascertaining,
your thoughts logical, though on a higher scale,
who can detect your intentions,
calculate your next upsetting move,
distinguish good from omnipresent evil,
since we are as grasshoppers in your sight?
    Dayenu.

In the morning you lift up princes,
in the evening you cast them down,

no task is beyond your execution,
no niche untouched by your love,
your words goad and refashion,
your silence like an alarm bell clangs,
your kindness fills to the brim, then overtops.
   Dayenu.

   II

Where were you, O man, when I hung up the solar systems to dry?
formed atmospheres conducive to elemental growth?
do you know the meaning of infinity
or what makes a baby cry?
which combination of atoms will prove fruitful or sterile,
the next world conqueror who'll arise?
I know—and, yes, I'm willing to elaborate.

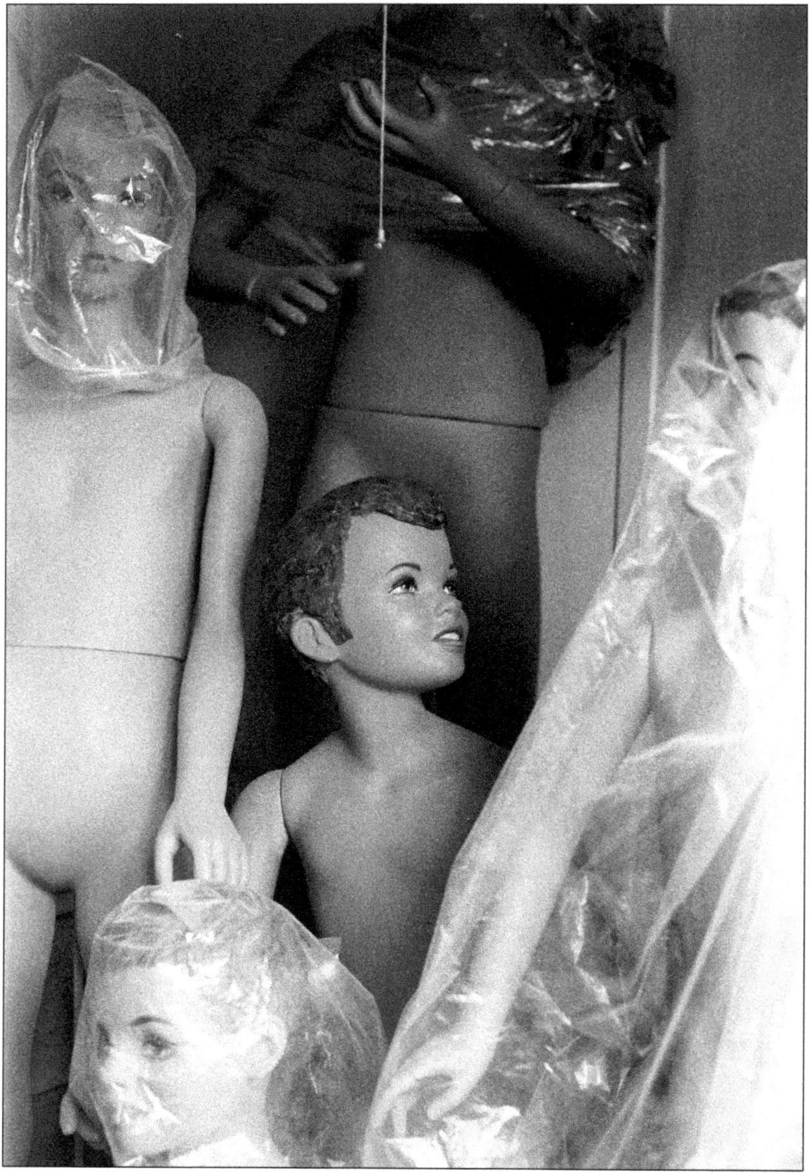

God Still Stands Indignant

God still stands indignant over those he is about to execute,
issuing last minute reprieves,
cushioning our pain with analgesic pills,
substituting second-degree burns in place of martyrdom,
tolling the chimes so all may turn and live.

Strangling misguided impulses,
detonating loud thunderclaps and potassium nitrates
above our bravado and conceit,
slicing our umbilical cords to tether *communitas*,
inundating us with unremitting downpours of mercy and grace.

Cranking up rusty, discarded motors, reactivating old power cells,
dropping flares above the sandboxes of precocious children,
pulling out the control rods to disturb our settled entropy,
pinching raw nerves, synchronizing our brains to our brawn,
restructuring nucleic acids to make a more perfect man.

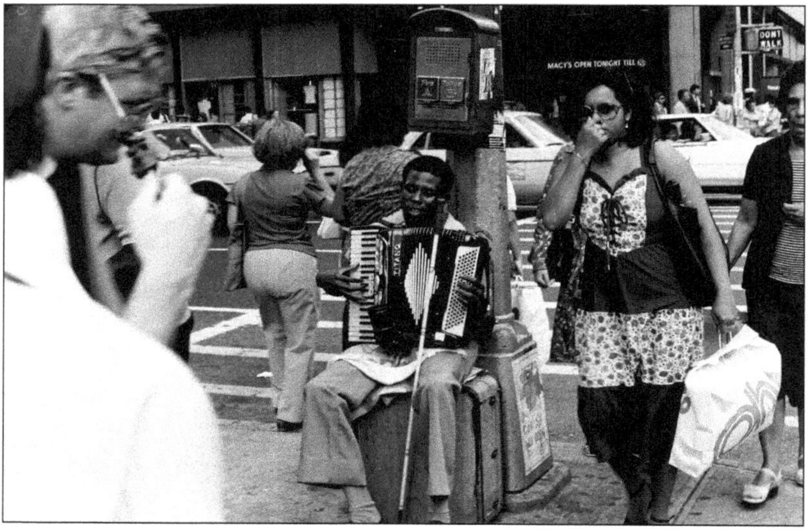
MACY'S OPEN TONIGHT TILL
DONT WALK

Here Come the Diminutive and Disfigured

Here come the diminutive and disfigured
followed by row after row of the deaf, the blind, the lame,
entire wards of psychopaths, schizophrenics,
the homosexual, the grotesque, the obese,
the indigenous, the multiracial, and the Romani,
the Sikh, the Baha'i, the Taoist, the Armenian, the Jew,
any with a lisp or deformity of any kind
are encouraged to undergo that shock therapy known as genocide
to purge us of bilious venom.

Any minority is prone to extermination
if pestilence breaks out,
barbarians bang at the gates,
usurpers insinuate themselves within the citadels of power;
to the slit-minded
all that's inexplicable
smacks of a conspiracy or a pact with the devil,
just as in Eastern thought blizzards, hail, drought, floods,
avalanches, volcanoes, the quaking crust itself
are the umpteen forms karma can take
to exact intergalactic justice.

Dangling by the neck from the scaffold,
penitents swing their Lazarus rattles
shouting "Unclean! Unclean!"
are anxious to confess any alleged crime,
since egregious culture fosters discrimination, pigeonholing,
only the wilderness can truly camouflage the outcast or scapegoat.

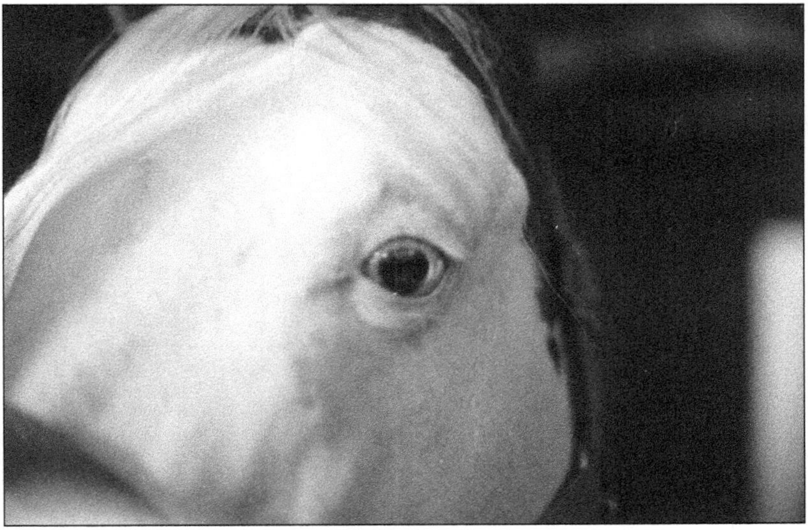

Golem

I am golem,
magnificent as the bronze horses
da Vinci never completed.

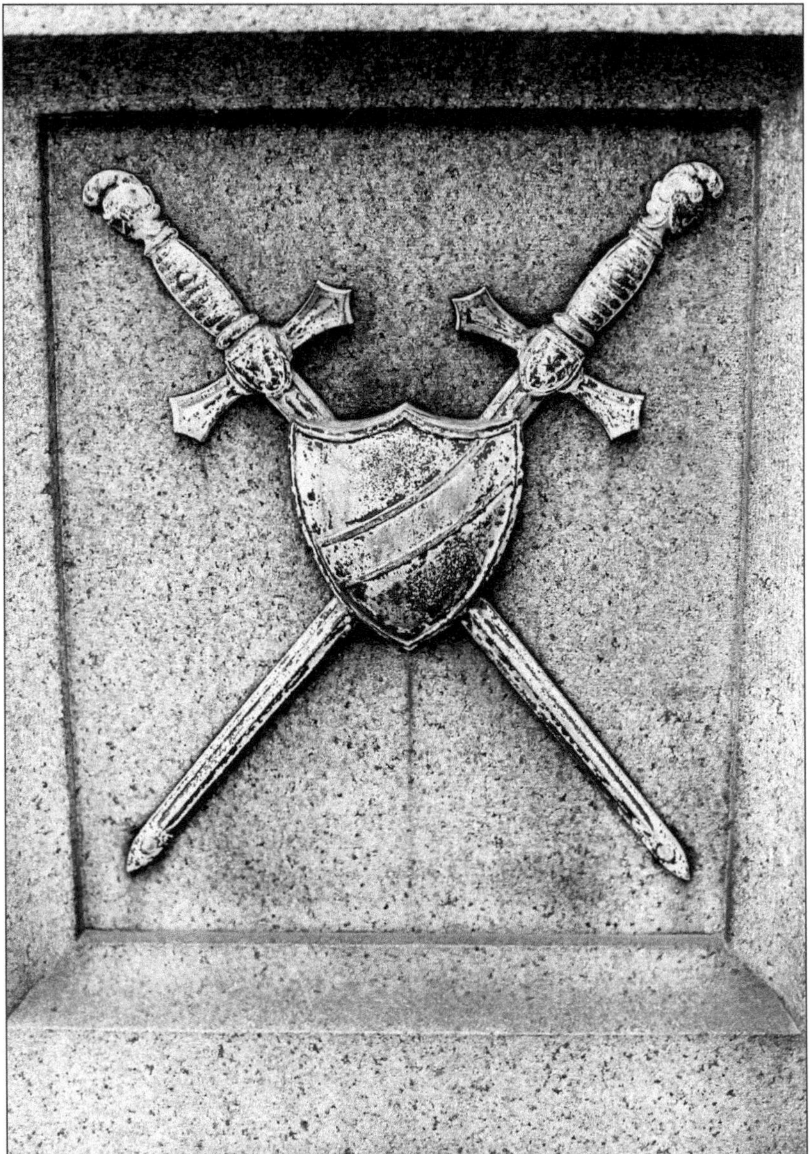

Monarchist Pretensions

David's star must rise,
Saul's sink below the Israelite horizon,
Messianic coat of arms
hail from a shepherd's pedigree,
inconspicuous Judah is elevated,
Joab pulls back from Uriah,
invincible with slingshot and plectrum,
our Orpheus relieves melancholic spirits,
banishes Ares to his wayward sons.

Abigail's peace offering—David's bandits accept,
wearing linen ephod, he dances before Michal and the ark,
throat-strangles the lion and bear,
100 Philistine foreskins crewel Saul's wall,
Nathan, his Tiresias, Bathsheba, almost his Jocasta,
by Absalom he's blinded,
monarchist pretensions mean exotic concubines,
standing armies, ongoing border disputes, aping
neighborhood pomp and circumstance.

The chronicler prefers a nomad's Arcadia
to grasping citified culture,
entangling alliances are the work of Baalzebub,
since YHWH, international arbiter, whistles for
sadistic Assyria, Sennacherib holds Hezekiah captive

like a bird in a cage. Floodgates are opened wide
for bribery, excessive tax burdens, egomaniacal tyrants
dependent on parroting toadies who vie
to be the first to publish "All's Well in Zion" panegyrics.

What if Moses wandered a Minotaur in
Ramses's labyrinth, parted the Erythraean Sea,
then returned to Memphis, wrote the Pentateuch
as a Spenglerian exercise in Qoheleth futility,
the manna evaporated before it touched your tongue,
Joshua quit after only six loops around Jericho,
Canaan blossomed, but with astringent herbs and sour cream?
So seven plagues upon you, city of David,
or at least goodly scourge and paradigm-shifting exile/captivity.

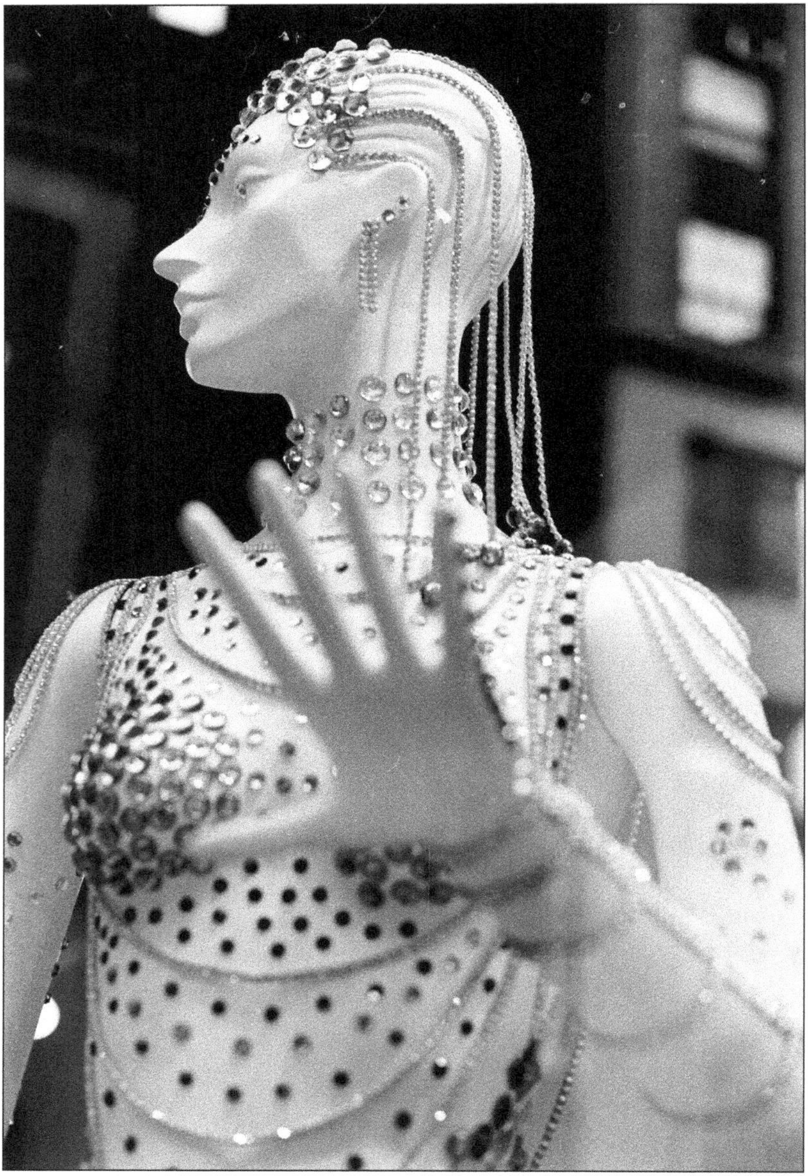

Ahab to Elijah

Have you come up against me, O my enemy,
with your diseased ravings and doomsday scenarios?
What have I done to incur the sting of your unstinting anger?

Cease all this babble about harlots washing in blood which dogs will lick up,
God knows we're created from fallible stock and makes allowances;
I admit to some mistakes, but your standards are wholly inflexible,
that odor of sanctity nauseating.

I'm too bound up with state dinners, grooming well-heeled successors,
building an ivory palace, laying out blueprints for Samarian cities,
ferreting out true prophets from camouflaged foes;
I've no inclination to attend your deeper life conventions.
Most demons are papier-mâché, Levitical codes one-dimensional;
ascetics I laugh at, penitents I feel sorry for.

So let's have less fire, more empathy, tolerance;
compromise is the essence of power.
Desert misogynist, return to your brooding oasis!
Are not others more dissolute, profligate, fingerers of *hamsa*;
for who doesn't clip the coin, clink the glass, covet vineyards,
gaze for a while at his neighbor's ewe?

We'll let history judge between us:
the stern, flamboyant pessimist or the far-sighted man of action—
which of us made Israel mighty and a force to be reckoned with?
And, you cad, leave my wife, Jezebel, out of this.

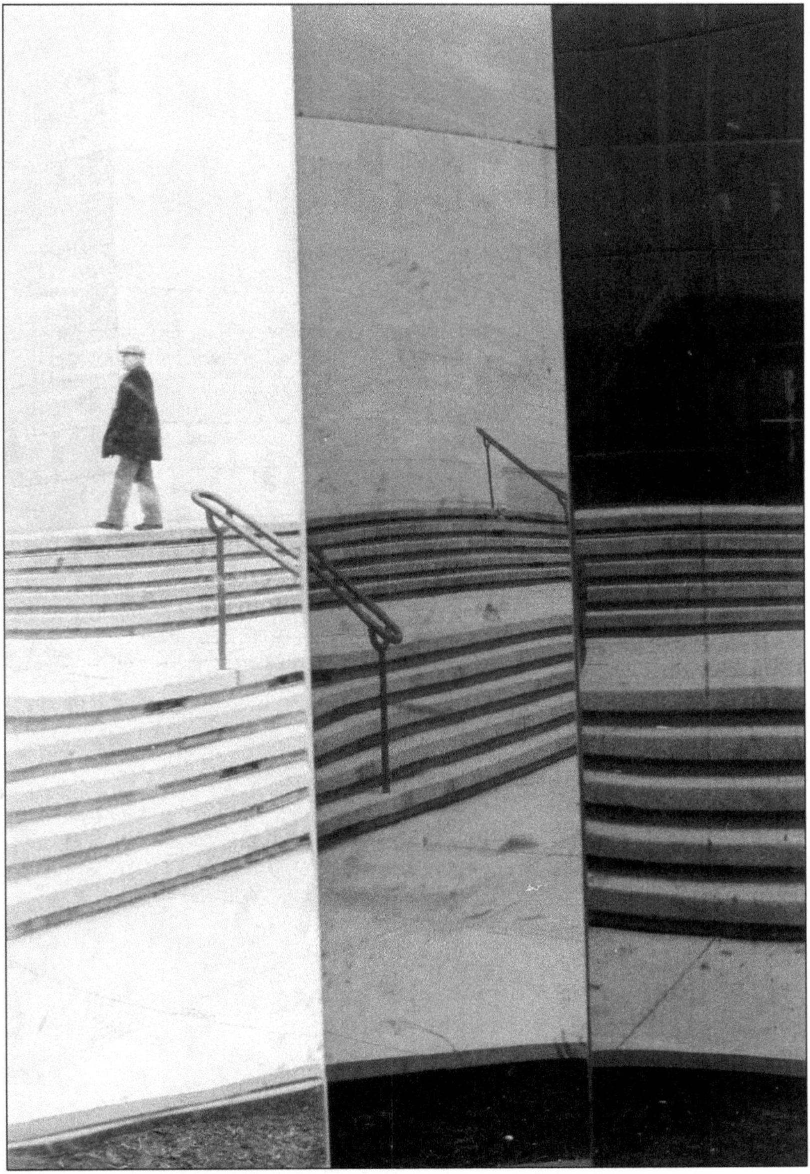

On Bonhoeffer's Participation in the Plot against Hitler

Conspiring against, and killing, wicked Amon
brought in good king Josiah,
perhaps the greatest reformer Judah ever knew.

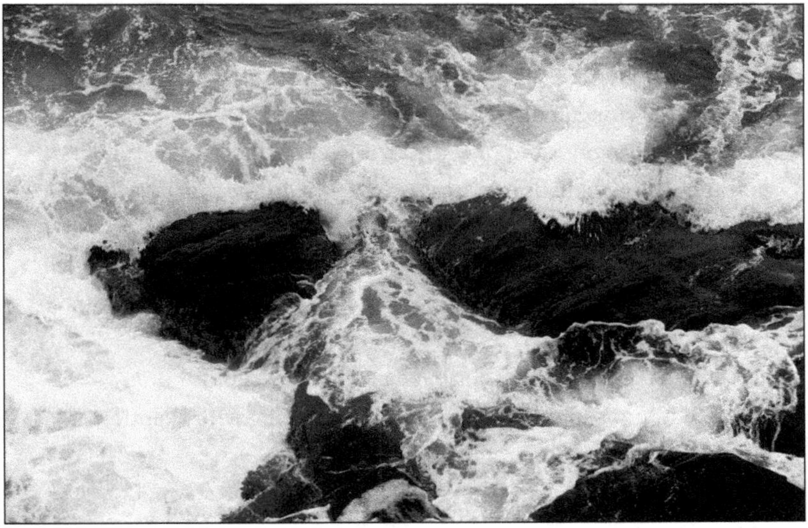

To Tarshish I Fly

To Tarshish I fly
to evade his elongated, probing fingers,
and there will I pipe and play the chameleon,
pulling from my knapsack: mascara, outlandish beards
    and mustaches,
so as to annul my call by feigning a fit of madness.

But should calamity strike
and superstitious sailors roll snake eyes for my soul,
and I be found supping with scoffers, conspiring with skeptics,
and my mind be hallucinogenic-bent,
lost in a whirlpool of churning illusions . . . .

Which type of contrition could ever purge,
what form of sacrifice prove efficacious?
If I were prodigal,
God would leap up to kiss and embrace,
but guilt clings to me tenaciously as an adhesive.

Instead of bounding down open-mouthed boulevards,
I'm caught in meandering goat paths, entwined in cul-de-sacs,
tottering under some scratchy signpost purporting:
    "This is Nineveh."

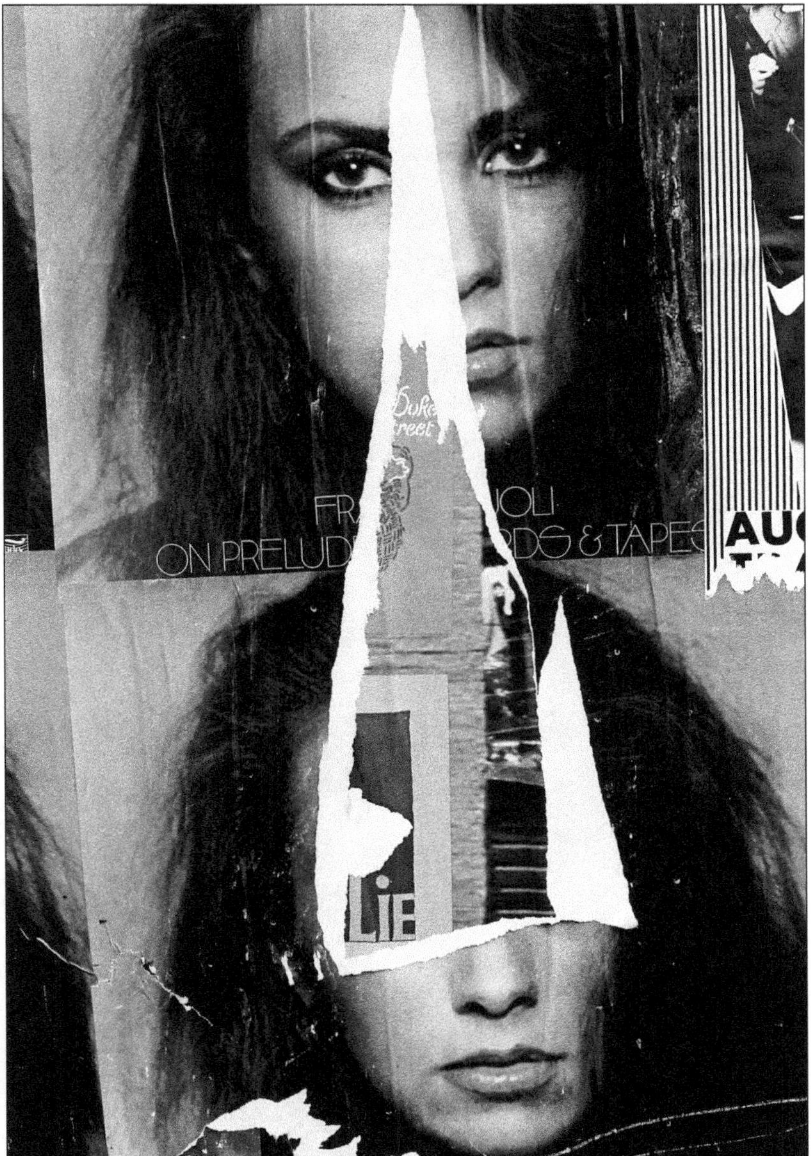
ON PRELUD
RDS & TAPES
LIE

A Ghoulish Gift

The Levite's dismembered concubine—
eleven presents to commemorate Benjamin's gang rape.

HYGRADE
FRANKFURTERS
ALL BEEF HOT CORN
HAMBURGERS FRENCH FRIES

Fractured Dreams

Ich bin der Geist der stets verneint![2]
("I am the Spirit that denies!")
—Mephistopheles in Goethe's *Faust, Part 1*

Believing fractured dreams
hatched by punitive imagination:
treachery, plots, unfaithful wives—
denigrating the outer real
for far-fetched, outsized,
macabre, exitless delusions;
collective fears, nightmarish excursions—
due to impotence, neglect or abuse—
warlocks, witches, bogeyman, moneyed Jewish councils,
grabs for territory or power;
the soul becomes enamored,
then debased, by what it loves.

This is the germ that infected and corroded
Hitler's childhood,
Stalin's incessant purges and gulag,
recant: admit what we *know*,
confessions can be obtained by truth
serums or Pavlovian torture—
the pliable brain must be regrooved.

2. Goethe, *Goethe's Faust*, 121, verse 1338.

Doctors test diabolical penal hypotheses
on unwilling "subhuman" victims;
the secret police round up the usual Kafkas
despite evidence that outright contradicts.

The mind is prone to dogma, absolutes,
airtight, sealed chambers
that admit no category known as "Error,"
the exceptions—denied—
stereotypes constructed out of ratcheting ghosts;
the illiterate rabble requires
iron rules and swift retribution,
tempered, of course, by grandiloquent,
feigned acts of mercy,
wink-signaling our Machiavellian intentions,
then denying all with charming, opposite-sounding words;
multi-layered, subjective everyday life
we unambiguously refuse.

Total destructive power feeds on the carrion
of corrupt, ego-fed dreams,
now that we're "older, wiser,"
mistaken for literal truth.

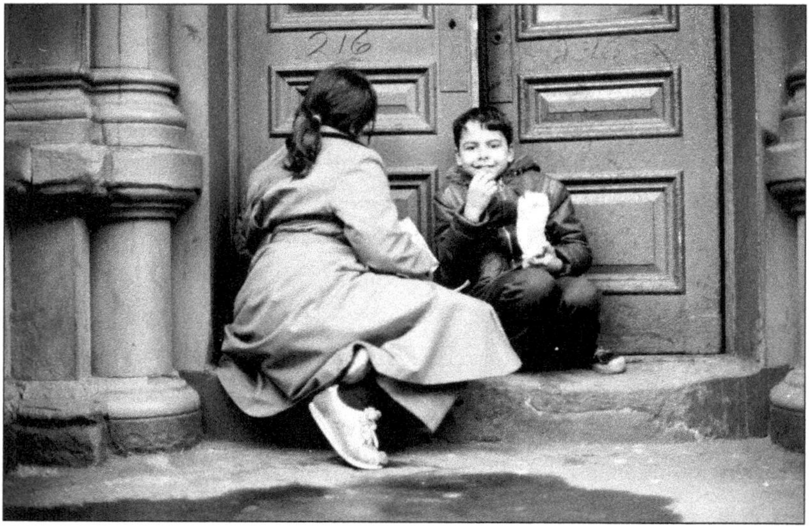
216

SS *Mutter*

Mother tucked us into iron rings,
then whispered a goose-stepping good-night.

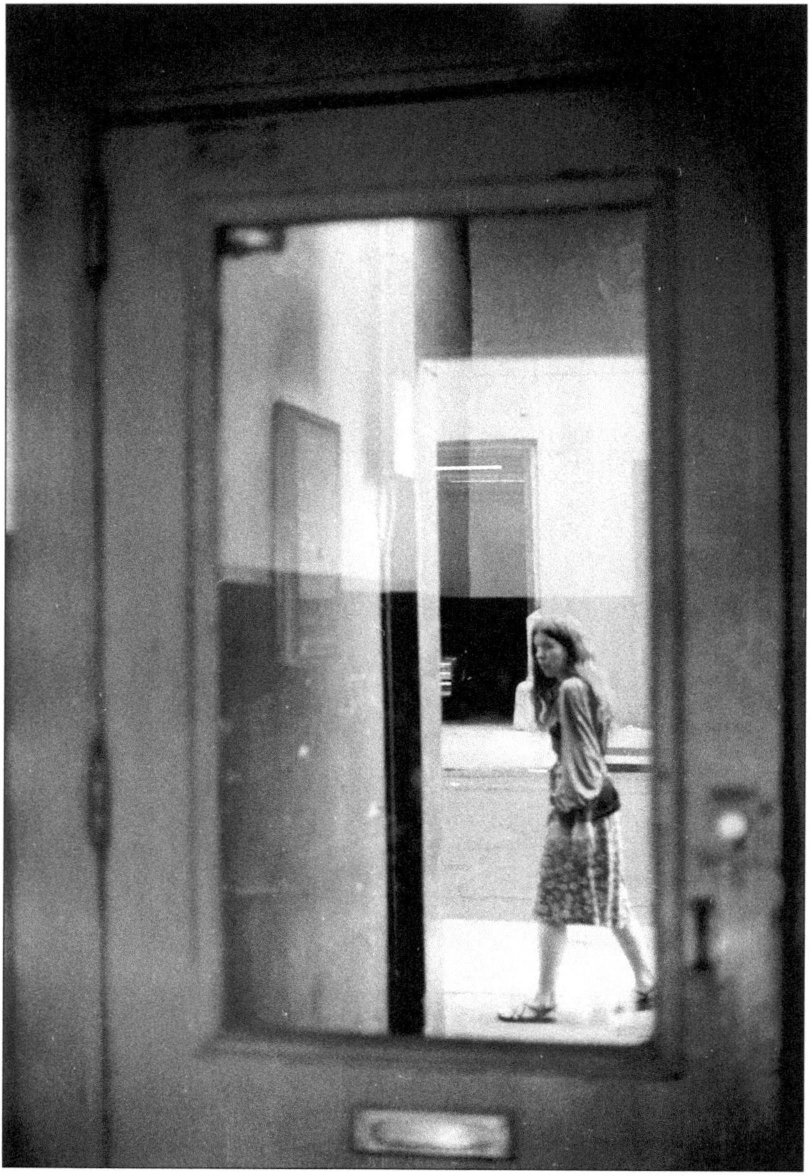

Eden

Into Paradise the serpent crept,
improbable decadent beauty—his last hurrah—
like a dying mafioso
whose last breath is revenge,
a subtle, scheming master
plotting intergalactically,
duping Eve, exaggerating the fruit
in Adam's mind,
will you doubt God's light command?
amid the perfumed flowers, singing birds, shapely trees,
man must learn once more
how to be naked and unafraid.

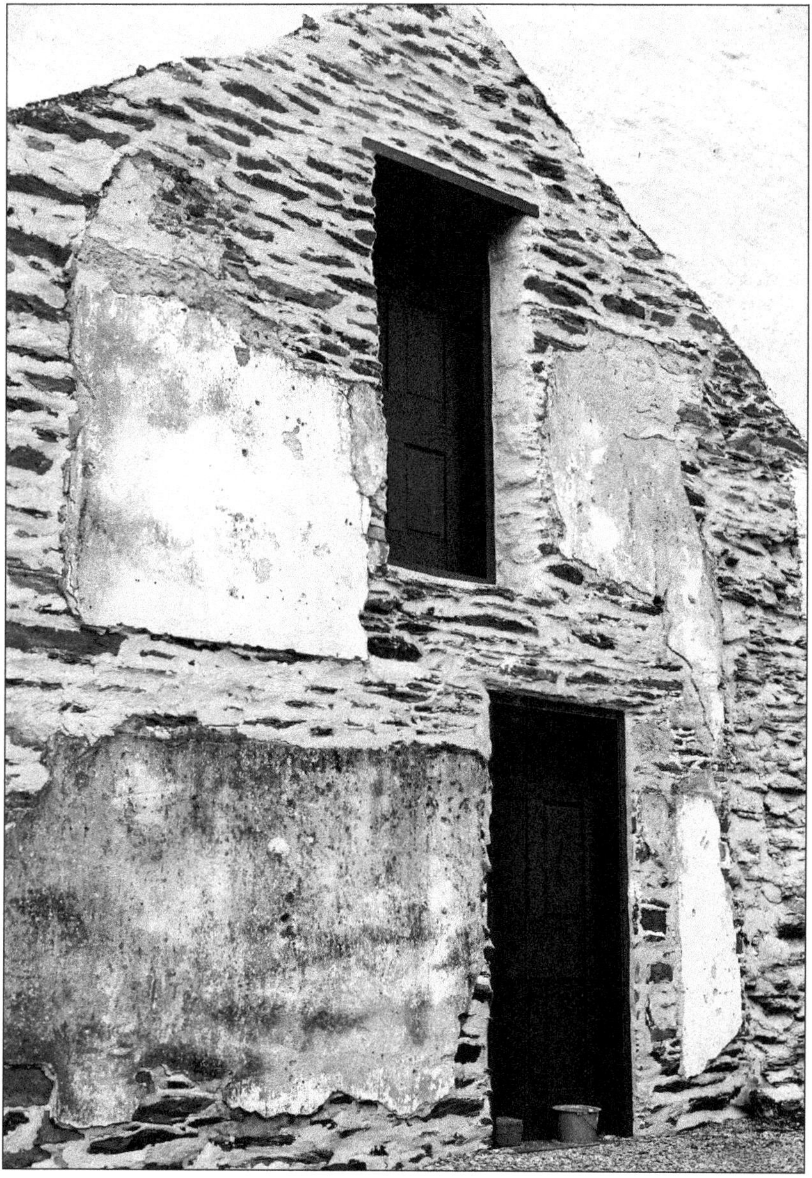

This Hermetically-Sealed Universe

I'm drawing nigh unto asphyxiation
in this hermetically-sealed, tripartite universe,
where exclusionary rules enforce endogamy
and the alien is quarantined like some rampant contagion.

Genius is too often stillborn or shrunken,
shriveled up by a searing bombardment of scorn,
the meanest flicker of eccentricity
risks expulsion; the tower; a yellow, emblazoned star.

Tolerance is to no advantage if ultra-orthodoxy reigns,
taboos are magnified into collective phobias, psychoses,
a chasm opens wide should one peer into forbidden recesses
or speculate on truths long revealed.

Congregations are held together by penitence, ablution,
    Seder meals,
as long as one acquiesces to the maxims of the fathers,
but should the canon be loosened,
accusations of apostasy, sorcery, and high-handedness flare up.

Accordingly, some feel more secure within a hidden canyon
than venturing out into the open plain,
perches, ledges can be defended by a loyal, elite cadre,
while rumor has it that the outlying expanses are under the sway
    of uncircumcised hordes.

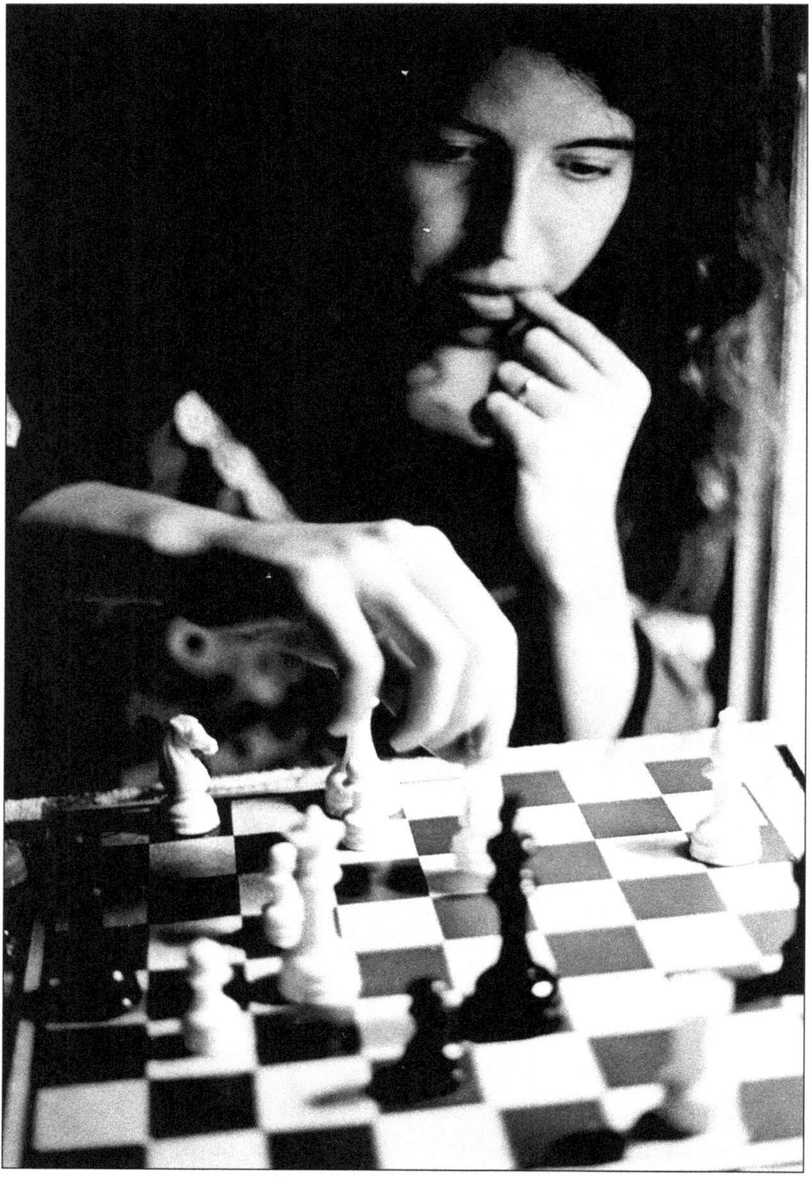

Am I Responsible?

Am I responsible
or has Heaven made me do it?
Will I come of my own volition
or am I predestined to salvation?
Shall Providence follow the general custom
or has she a more fastidious mind?
Are all things good or evil
or do some fall in between?
Is God in pitched battle
or has the accuser capitulated?

I raise the questions
without an adequate reply.
Shall "accident" and "luck"
be relegated to recycle bins,
"fate" and "determinism"
be expunged from our prehistoric past:
Clotho, Lachesis, and Atropos?
Or is vocabulary the problem,
awkward phrases wrung from hazy thought?

To be or not to be—
an illegitimate question
because it lacks a subject?
Can we call "catastrophe"
what God meant to be a boon to the human race?

Is "affliction" a synonym for "jubilation"?
Do atoms swerve occasionally
or does divine Reason foreordain?

Logic is a faithful tool
for those who judge it rightly.
But Spinoza and John Calvin,
I beg of you, reconsider,
language is more than tautology and self-contradiction.
The positivists have honed your words
into meaningless categories.
Observe: in such a world
what need have we for poets?

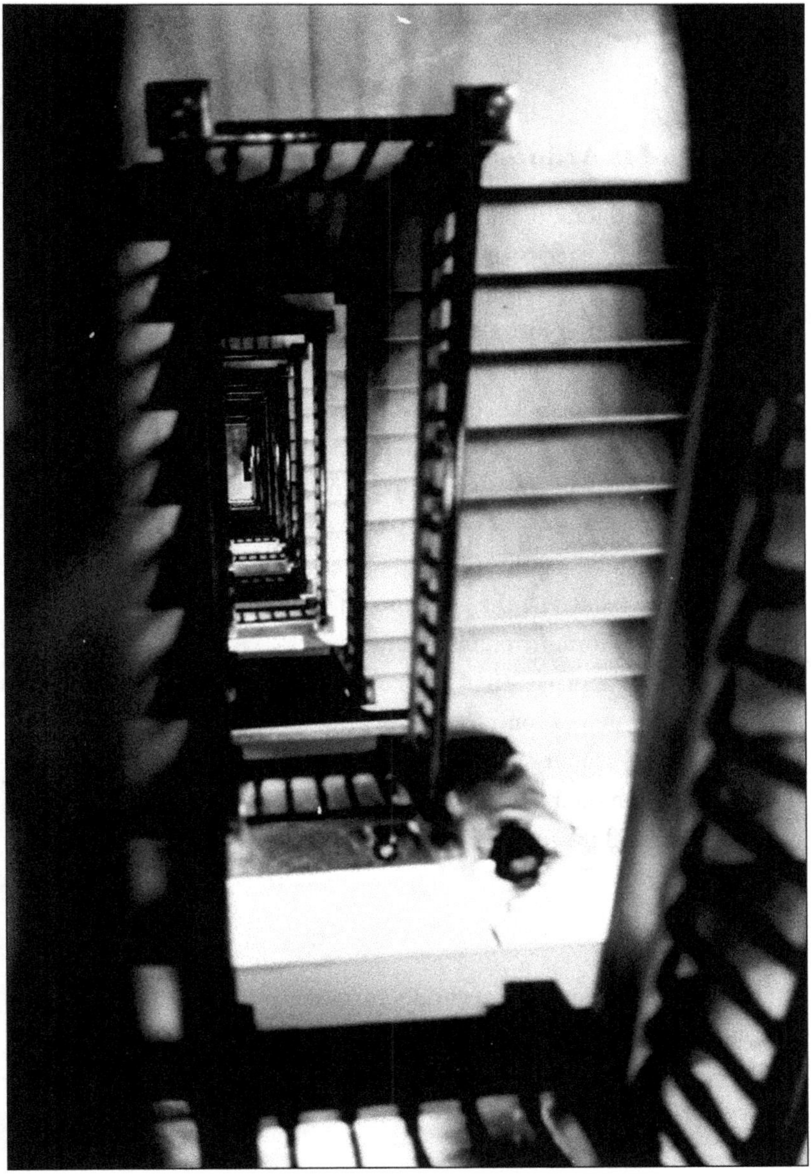

The Road Is Arduous

The road is arduous, the obstacles self-replicating,
I stub my toe on each grain of sand,
the horizon is no nearer than the day I first set out,
decisions encounter turbulence, side winds,
strong/weak/gravitational/electromagnetic forces
hinder the equanimity I had hoped to achieve,
the forks, the bends, the loop-to-loops make my balance wobbly,
imperceptibly I reach for a vanishing hand.

Unsure of my true psychic identity, I internalize my accuser,
then become fixated on the ten *sefirot* of the Kabbalah,
sensing a tepid timidity on my right,
while on my left, maelstroms whirl up from the pit,
anti-me's threaten to contract-implode,
rice paddies resemble soggy minefields,
enemies put on their smiley-faced masks, God tugs
at the pillars till the foundations begin to shake.

II

I envy those with exuberant childhood dreams,
compression-tension forces seek to shatter my spans,
cracks, fractures dislocate the highest beams,
I keep propping up the weight-bearing arches,

buttressing the main thoroughfares,
but the structural flaws are endemic,
the raw materials isomorphically unstable,
while the trusses run parallel to the grain and continue to weaken.

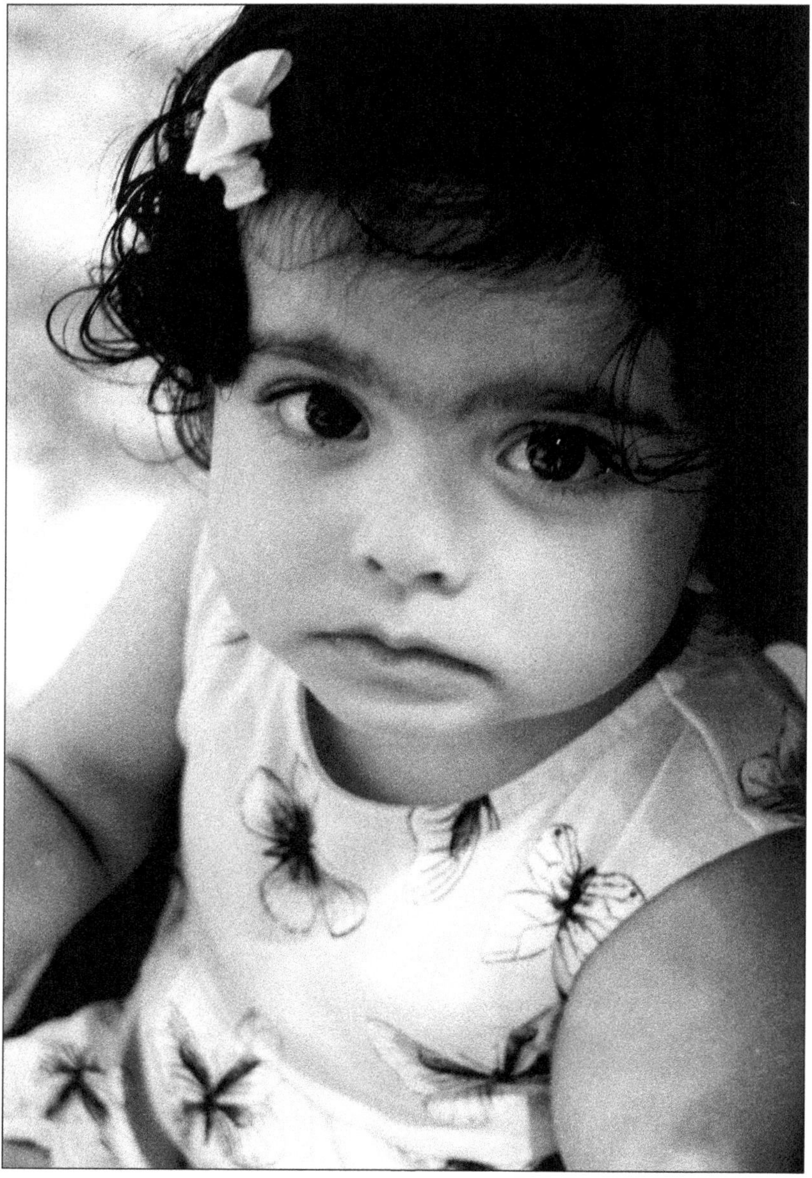

Transitions

Transitions, rites of passage,
through one door and out the other,
all knotted up, we hesitate, forebodings
of fabulous, phantom places
stalk our every step,
beyond the Pillars of Hercules
are red-hot pokers, Dogon masks,
ghouls, Furies, fiends.

Adventurers are lured by thoughts of booty,
scholars set out to prove a cherished thesis,
but how to move these kosher rams
from the loading chute
into a more easterly direction
requires a Ph.D. in subtler persuasion,
so I nudge a little, hang out a carrot,
supplicate, allow colleagues to add a word of encouragement.

But this synagogue is prey
to mass charismatic movements, high-pitched fevers,
bigoted appeals to patriotism—they
march from one stupid bugler to another false alarm,
I wring my hands at their delusions,
set fire to their golden calves, denounce
Molech, Ashtoreth, and that ugly Hydra,
Baal, the master hypnotist.

II

How painful to transgress from child
to woman, from goo-goo toys to puberty,
from serf to freedman, liberations
uncork Orwellian tremors, stir up a murky pudding,
—things one would just as soon avoid—
I'd rather spend my day with Lego blocks and Esther dolls
than assume the status of a Bat Mitzvah girl.

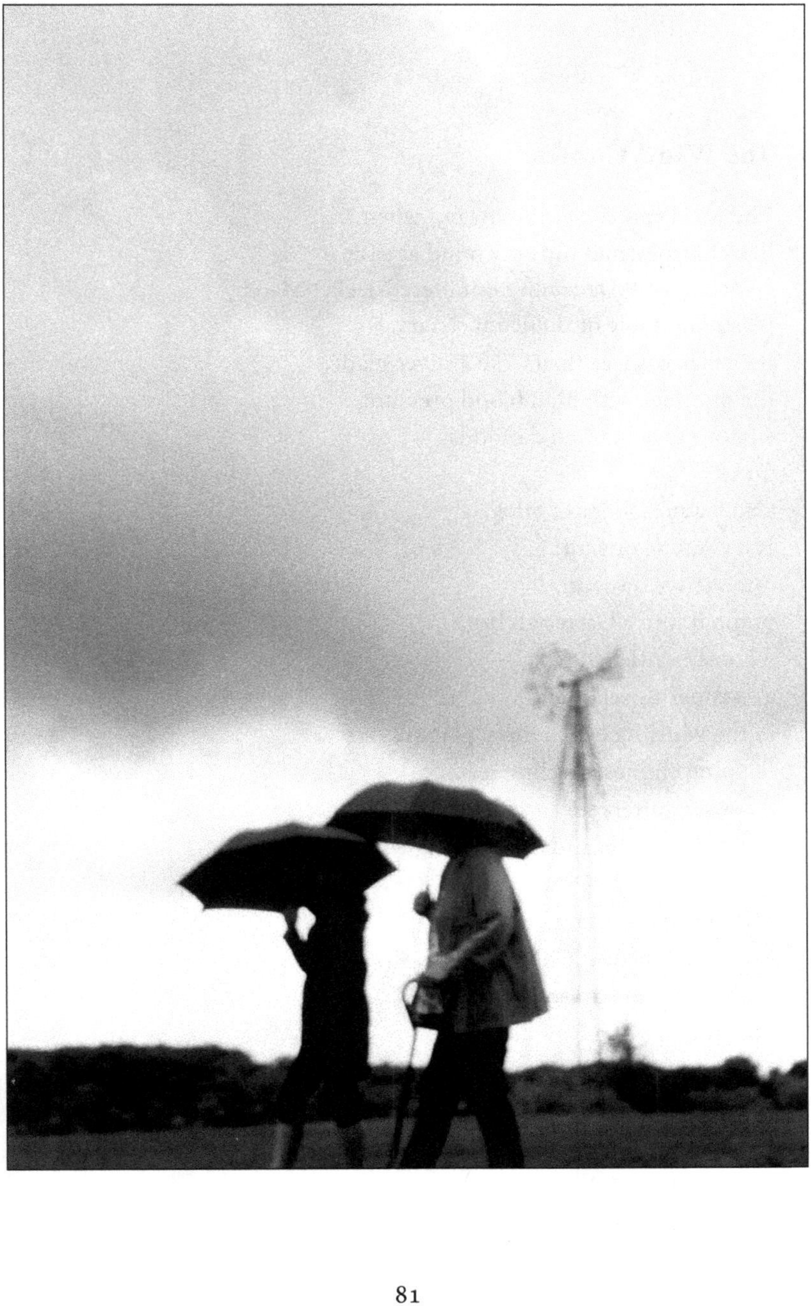

The Wind Comes

The wind comes, yet I know not when,
like chloroform it puts my mind at ease,
cemetery-still December or tattered-jacket March,
jet stream sable or doldrum canary,
the albatross free floats like a silver blade,
the hummer with high blood pressure
siphons love-starved daffodils.

Catch a mason jar of ether,
is it alkaline or acid?
radioactive or neutral?
pump it into a Cartesian bag,
whoosh! rattle! click!
a summer tinsel or autumnal thud,
in the whirling eye there's a place of peace,
flapping chimes, tinkling reeds,
a bowler guttered by a zephyr,
gnarled junipers and the whining willow.

The *pneuma*—Adam's respirator—
wheezes out when Gabriel blows,
gushing about Samson's jawbone,
galvanizing King David's lyre,
Marduk exhales, Isis speaks,
Yahweh's funnel-shaped *ruah*,
even so, come, glossolalia
as fire, water, or oil,
but without Montanist excess.

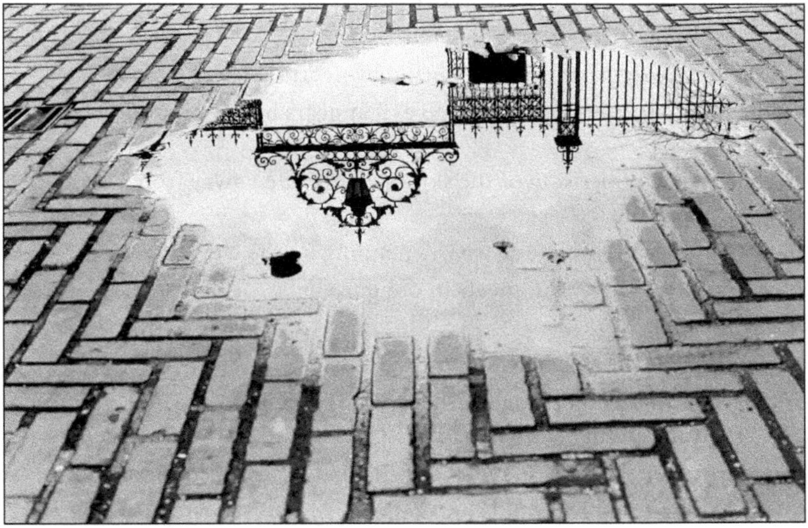

Geometric Figures in Whimsy

The line of demarcation is trisected by neutral zones,
the boundary between good and evil appears blurry around
 its edges,
the vertical dimension of the skyscraper is tilted away from
 the horizon,
do latitude and longitude vary depending on the elevation?
our love is circular but meets in oblique angles.

Two parallel lines slowly lose their distaste,
the trapezoid and pentagon are closed figures, but can you locate
 their midpoints?
a dot, a French whorl, an ellipse—what have they in common?
a parabola and a hyperbola are conic sections,
yet one curls us up to heaven, the other mires us in purgatory.

In Ptolemy the exceptions are not the rules,
so why does Copernicus throw out the geocentric world?
though a diagonal can intersect at any angle it pleases,
the inner and outer arcs of the parallelogram total 360°,
epicycle follows after epicycle in consecutive, repeatable
 proportions.

Two magnetic axes tug on iron particles,
the nearest cling with sheer delight,
while those more distant tip their hats and gaze,
L'Enfant's Washington radiates like a starfish around its
 White House core,
while Paris takes its donkey routes as pure, inspired growth.

The ouroboros stands for humanity coiling up its apotropaic rod,
earth is a rectangular toy box participating in perihelion games,
heaven, a curiosity cabinet suffused with counterpoint tête-à-tête,
and God, well God, is the focus and the pioneering periphery,
a checkerboard maze as absurd as the wing-to-body ratio of
   a domesticated silkworm.

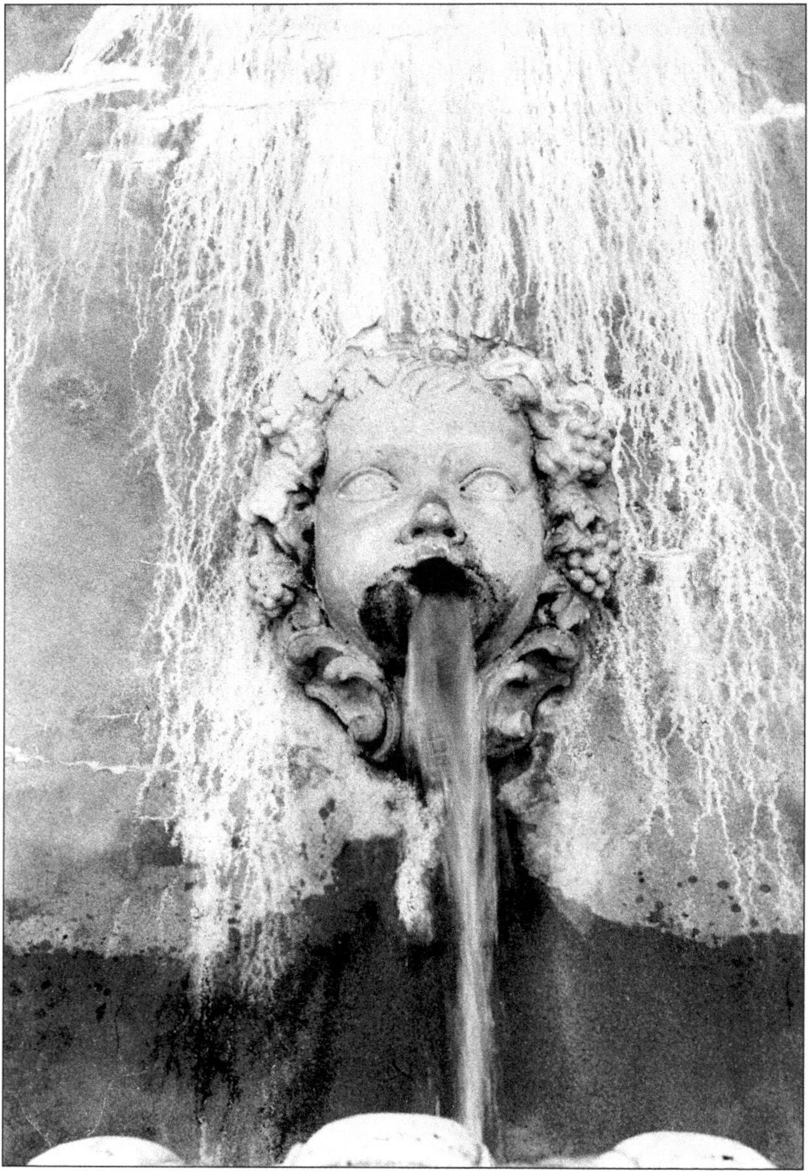

Wet vs. Dry

Were I to count the total of all the tears shed
since Adam ate the sickly fruit,
the upper atmosphere would be humid 100%,
rainforests would sprout over vast sections of the Sahara,
plants evolve having vacuole drains,
man comes born in his own wet suit.

Salt water is good,
remorse carries the seeds of repentance,
blessed are those who sow and weep,
for they'll reap with bubbling joy,
just as the mourners at Enoch's funeral rose up to sing and dance,
God himself will wipe away each tear.

A remnant (those who are contrite) will be released from
　Babylon's prison,
while the prince of the air shivers, albeit with an unchiseled,
　defiant heart;
at the first hint of rain,
his demons evacuate the premises,
a conscience-stricken David throws a pall over their puerile souls,
a kneeling, downcast publican induces guilt in any
　sympathetic onlooker.

But Satan is stoic to the end,
resigned, but unbowed.
Deception when enfleshed is never truly self-critical,
his army consists of legions of sadist second lieutenants,
whether sin, guilt, peace—lamb, bull, or ram—
should they make an offering, it can never burst into flame.

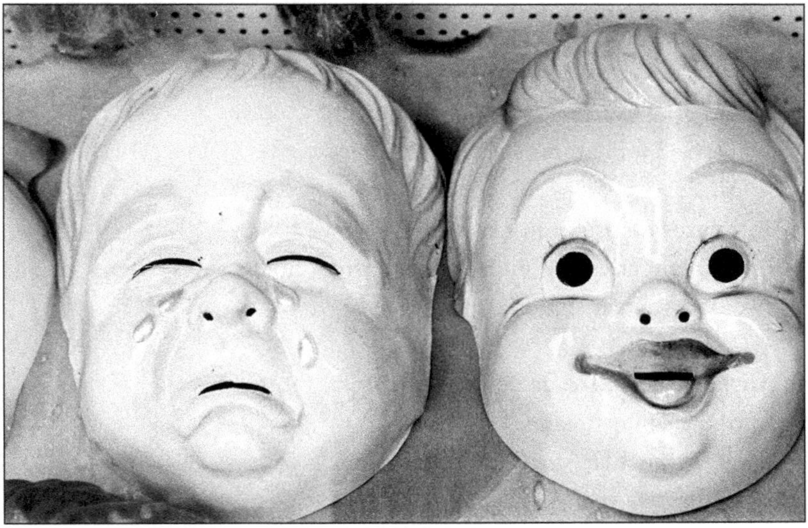

Tears: Nature's Safety Valve

When tears well up for the umpteenth time,
    and grief overflows our puny dams,
thank God for nature's safety valve.

A spouse falls asleep in Abraham's bosom,
    an infant cries "ma-ma" for the very first time,
two tribes at war sign a lasting peace.

Then let them cascade down your cheeks,
    rivulets into streams,
a watery sanctuary for released emotions.

A tear is God's gift to his hell-bent people,
    dew sparkling in the Devil's playground,
a *zeugma* of liquid grace.

Life appears as a mixed blessing to the children of Eve,
    every smile dissolved into a frown,
each joy ephemeral—salt water quickly washed away.

Passions break through our surface pores
    in bubbles of purgation,
Spartan facade unmasked by a moist epiphany.

Involuntary reflexes causing just alarm
   that we are not so resolute
as Seneca or the granite of New Hampshire.

Yet flow they must,
it is Nature's own law,
aftereffect of shock,
precursor of Heaven,

Either grieve now
or never know laughter.

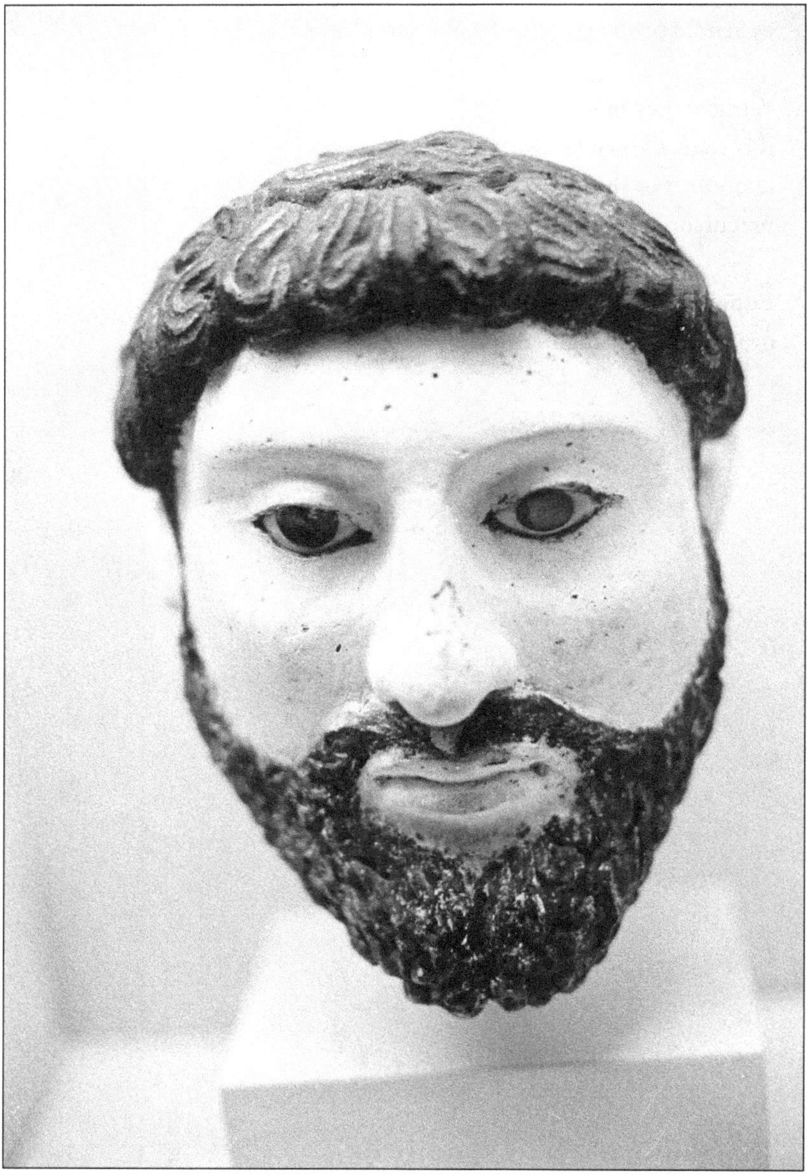

Exodus 28: Twelve Tribal Stones

Twelve tribal stones on Aaron's breastplate
to remember Israel always,
blue pomegranates and gold bells,
the nation's guilt on his atoning forehead.

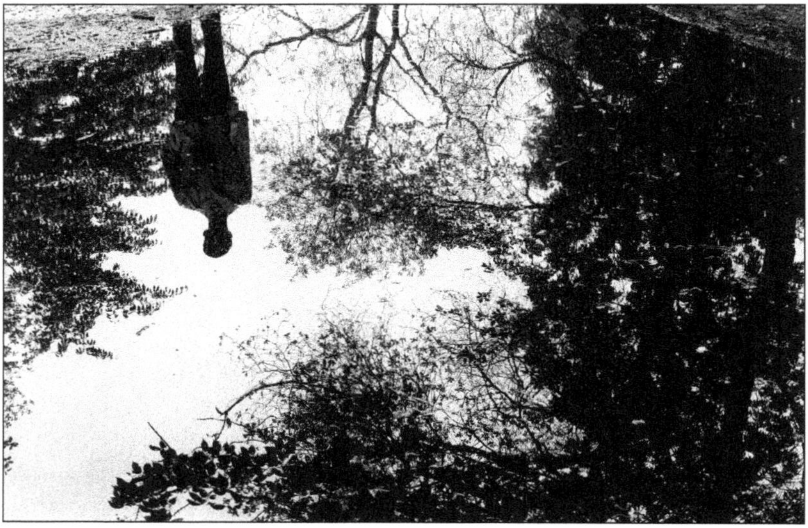

Notes from My Nervous Breakdown

I can't quite pull myself together,
stuffing falls out of my ragamuffin head,
though I keep shoving it back in as fast as I can,
I shuffle past half-open doors and shuttered windows,
my ego is withered,
friendly greetings turn ominous, thundering,
neutral gestures glower mean as glass,
slights I once overlooked
loom hurtful under my magnifying lens,
who could possibly recognize this crumbling man?

I question stability, tightrope maintain a demented balance,
yet how shall I continue on
when every doorpost reads "Failure!"
every street sign calls out, "You Fool!"
onlookers gawk and shake their tresses,
I've become known as a reckless lance corporal
who cuts off every conceivable avenue of escape.

I spar, exaggerate, say more than I ought to,
imagine patently absurd possibilities,
believe conspirators are plotting my forthcoming demise,
feel God wants to trip me up, then laugh out loud,
my family may know, but they refuse to acknowledge the real diagnosis,
for the consequences are too fraught with dread,
so they put on a merry bluff.

I'm tottering,
latch onto filaments, reeds,
anything that offers a modicum of support,
people don't call up
because they're offended, disgusted,
letters go ploddingly unanswered
because all see through my cleverest ruses
—it's over except for the funeral.

Steady she goes,
beware that Antarctic ice,
the shoals are directly leeward,
yet with a fortuitous combination of tailwinds and good timing,
I can still right this nearly-capsized schooner,
start the bilge pumps churning,
should I have the will and Pelagian stick-to-itiveness.
keva and *kavanah*.

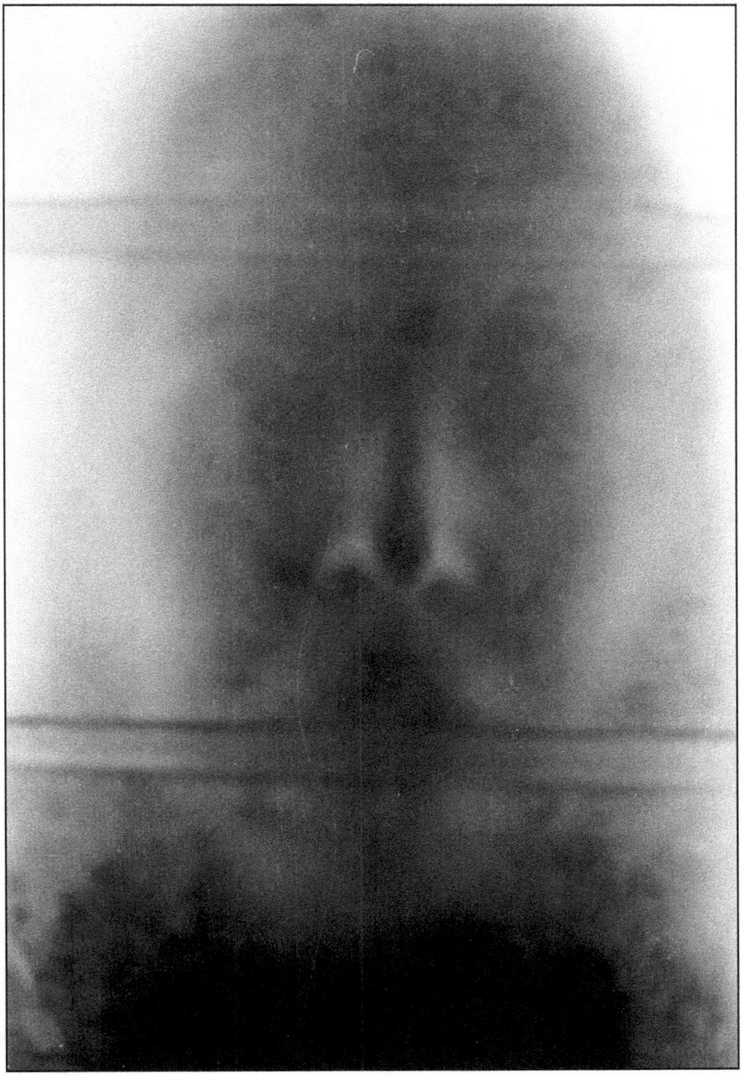

The Wart of God

Why should I take note
   if Afric' starves
and Archduke Ferdinand is dead,
   I am the wart of God,
others constitute his fingers—
   the world can hum along without me.
I am the appendage
   man should have evolved beyond,
which interns routinely sever
   to make a little pocket change,
I am the hammer
   whose head was twisted on upside down
that carpenters throw out or write off for a loss,
   I am the resistance
to momentum or progress,
   the inertia that
keeps lost satellites in space,
   I am the circuit
lacking but a switch,
   the summer fungus
with no known rationale,

    the evil that exists
to contrast with the good,
    the poison
which has no antidote.

Do I sound as if a wire's loose?
    PLEASE REPAIR
    THIS ROBOT.

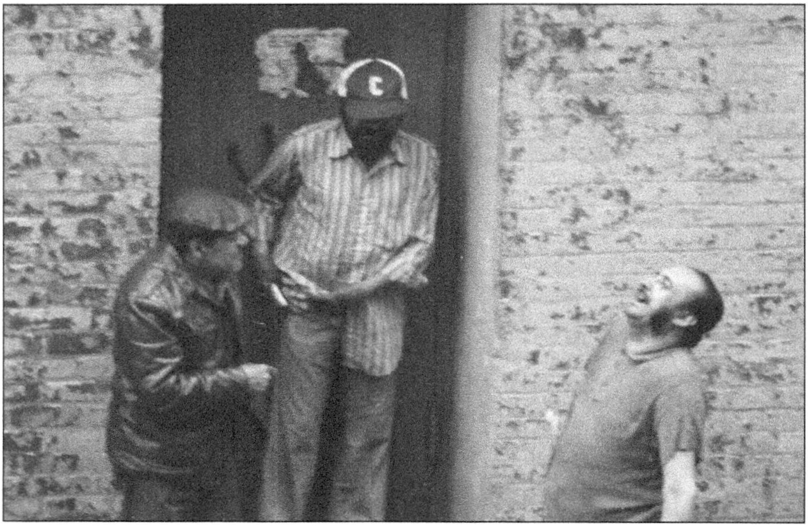

Wagging Manikin Faces

"Contend, O Lord, with those who contend with me."
—Psalm 35:1

Wagging manikin faces
that jeer and frown,
snickering, pernicious smiles
which curl up in cool disdain,
jointed fingers which stab, accuse,
teeth that white howl,
a nose, snubbing and twitching.

I'm encircled by maddened bullies,
tossed about on their makeshift trampoline,
like some "dumb" blond, paralyzed, near to being gang raped,
they paw at my shirt, slash my strings,
from their mouths pour forth withering slurs,
with arms locked behind my neck,
they manhandle, emasculate, abuse.

Friends—stinking cowards—won't intervene,
the heehawing crowd shouts,
"Who was it slugged you? Fondled your behind?
Effeminate! Mama's boy! Pushover!
Where are your braggart curses now?"

Once pommeled, my head smashed against the pavement,
nose bleeding into my underwear,
I picked up what pieces remained,
dusted off and salved the inordinate bruises,
struggled home: mangled, disillusioned, sliced open,
who could live after such shame?

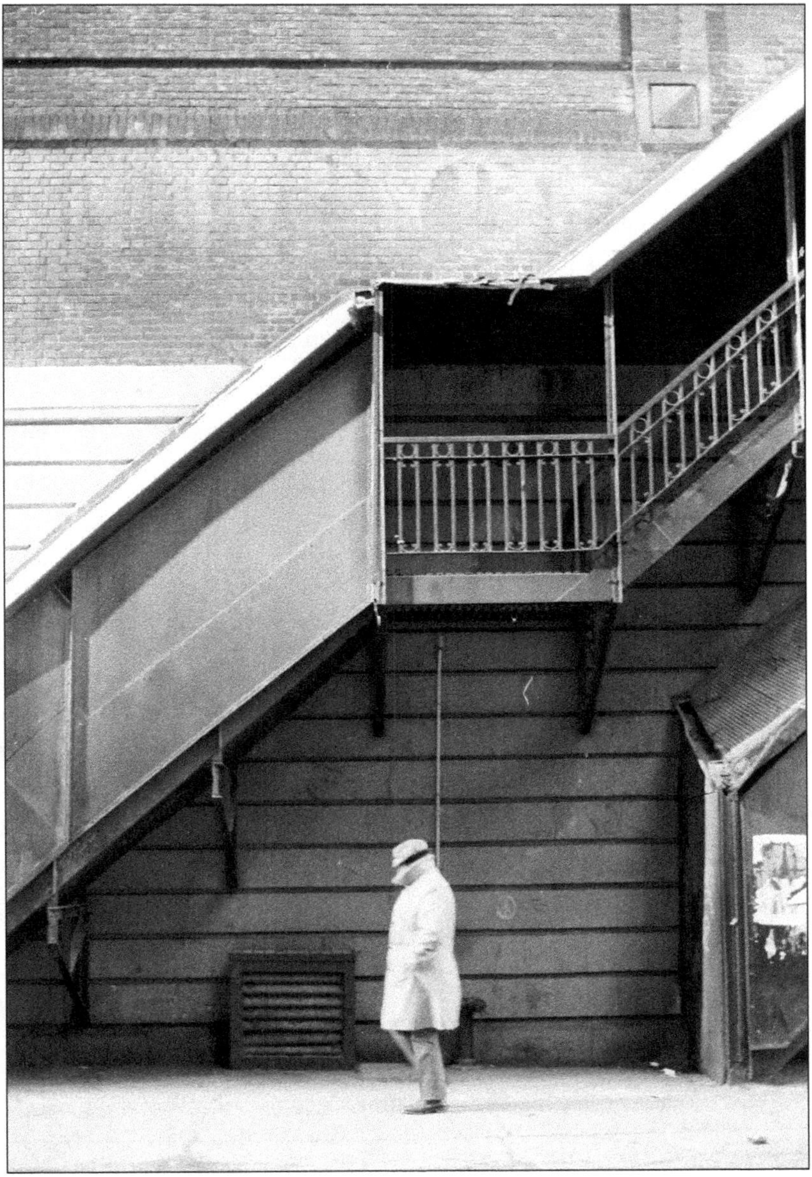

Jacob's *Kuntz*

At Jabbok, there my identity changed,
I, who had been known as the arch con-man/manipulator,
protested against my alter ego,
as having been interwoven in fraudulent culpability,
shut in by base, accusing voices.

I awoke: maimed, shivering, alarmed,
how could I hope for reconciliation
after lo, these many deceptive years,
since notorious I had conspired with my own mother
to steal the firstborn's blessing?

Would Esau now accept a mere pittance, a bribe?
Suppose I admitted to an auxiliary role in the intrigue,
allowing that I myself had been half-duped?
forced to put on rawhide armlets,
cook a venison stew?

I stammer, limp, am now atrophied,
still, I am one who strives,
but shall I ultimately prevail?

105

A Little Yiddish Humor

You shall not tattoo an Assyrian,
clip off a Mede's ear,
hire an Edomite as belly dancer for your father's funeral,
put a Moabite in a cistern,
tempt Philistines to carnival.

You shall not wear tassels during Av, Passover,
remove a hermaphrodite's goatee,
wear satin and twilled cotton in the same undergarment,
savor fermented plums in a barley field,
throw up your excrement before the Lord.

You must not allow those whose testicles have been crushed
to implant impious seeds within Israel's borders,
permit a bastard to sing baritone in the temple choir
or uncover the lewd intentions of your lascivious mother—
lest she make a troika of her debauchery.

You shall not put felons in gopher wood stocks
unless two or three children agree to hurl acorns and tomatoes,
sign a pact of surrender with those the Lord wishes you
   to exterminate,
allow a harlot to visit an imbecile,
yoke a piebald ox to a striped buffalo.

Those born with a congenital lisp
should be fed to lockjaw tigers,
when you surround an enemy camp gouge out only the eyes
    of the pacifists,
institute 1200 cities of refuge
so the unbeliever can flee from the ultra-orthodox's fury.

You shall never lend at or below the prevailing rate,
cook barracuda and haddock over the same open pit barbecue,
offer a sickly goose as a peace offering,
put a golem in charge of the king's infantry,
remove the ancient landmarks except to encroach upon
    goyim borders.

Where there is a dispute between a male and a female,
neither shall grab the other's private parts in full view of gaping
    neighbors,
rather each should be seated calmly behind thin, translucent
    curtains,
then like pornographic Balinese puppets
have at the other's charcoal shadows.

If any of your manservants or maidservants has an ecstatic,
    millennial vision,
orates like Philo on the One's oceanic goodness,
lead, escort, kick him from your midst,
may his descendants be cursed until Messiah comes
or they openly acknowledge God's sovereign, mercurial wrath.

If anyone communes with demons,
conjures up Lilith, Perizzite spirits, the witch of Endor,
that man we know to be both a liar and a *navi*,
whatever he says the people must do
to purge any remnant of good left in reprobate Israel.

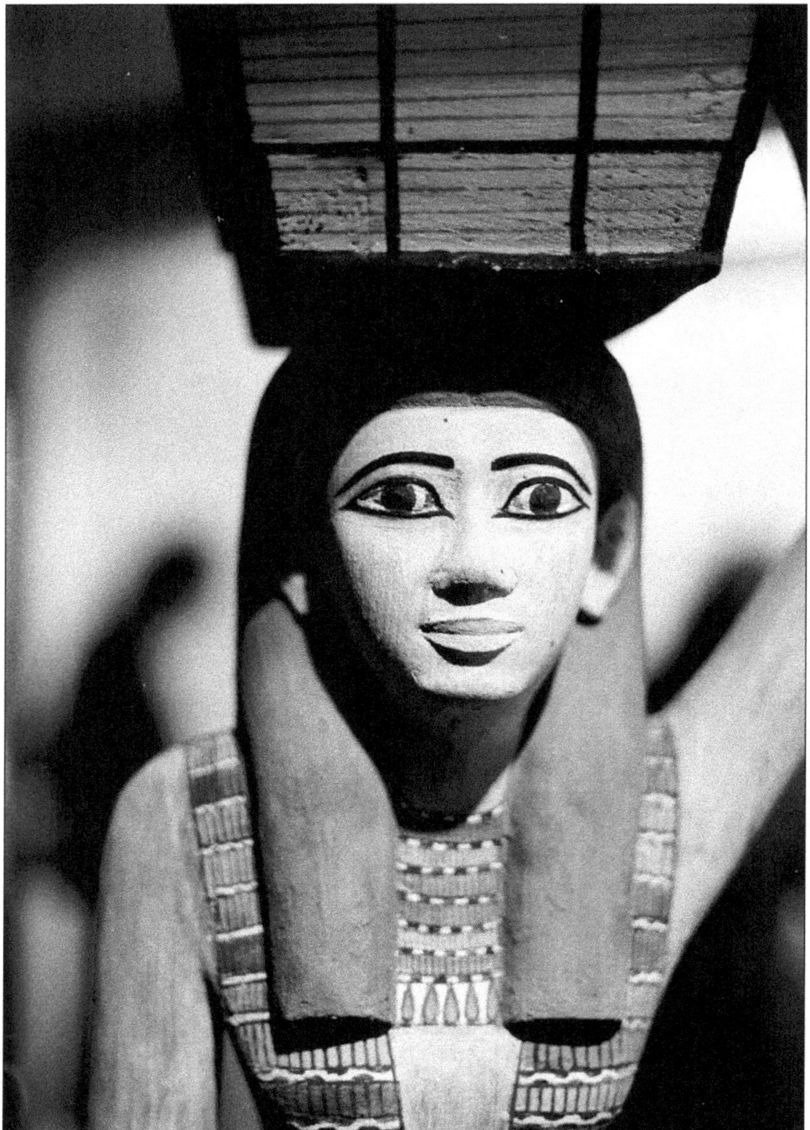

Joseph

Where is that dreamer:
devoured by some wild beast
or gone off to Egypt
hot for Potiphar's wife?

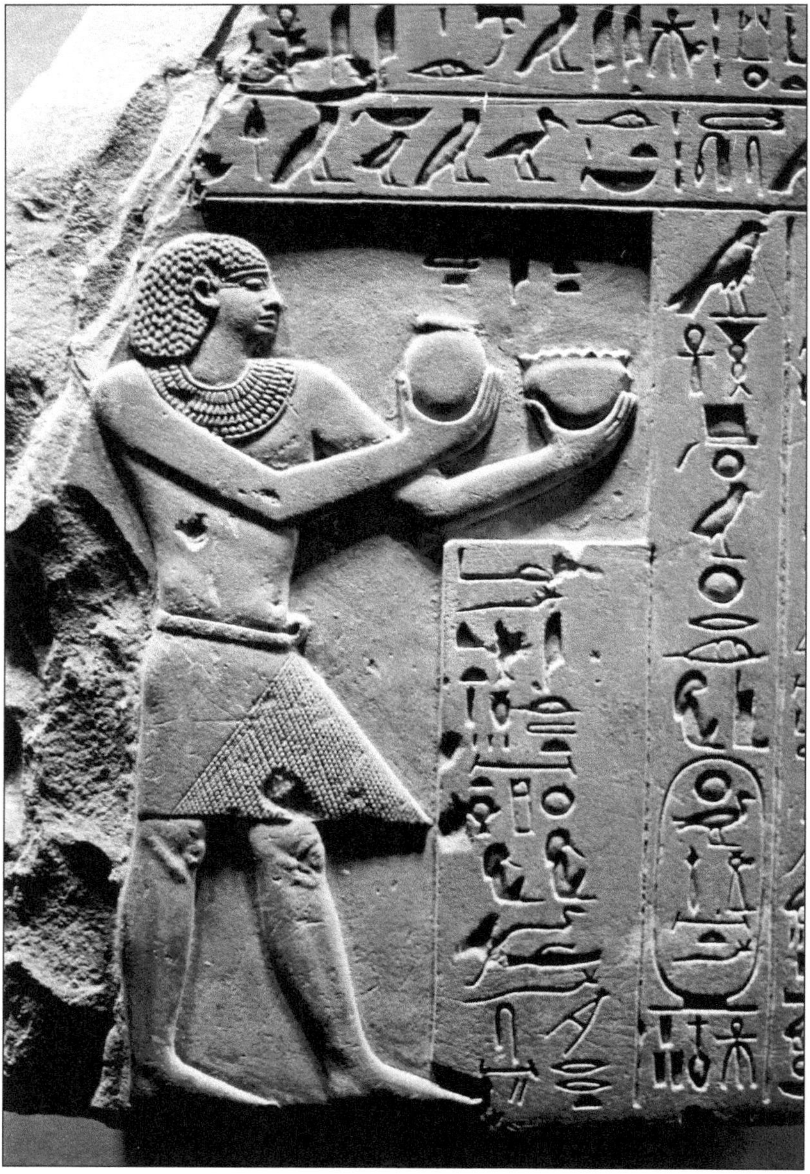

Yahweh vs. Horus

Aaron's rod gulped down
the entire Egyptian pantheon,
burped up one or two lesser deities.

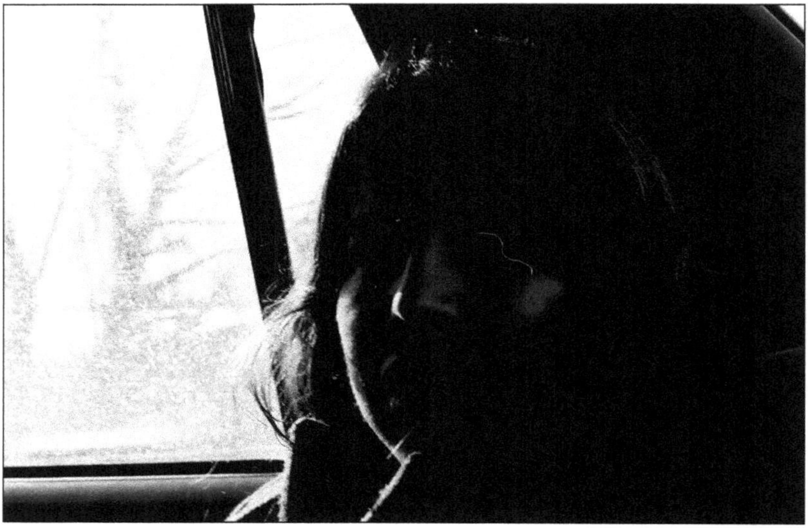

You Have Become My Enemy

You have become my enemy, O Lord,
who once were a friend;
your silence stiffens,
even dew no longer forms beneath your granite heavens,
taciturn echoes recede,
all that's left are intertestamental relics
and a petrified storehouse of saints' miracles,
wonders that could never be duplicated
in this faithless age of bronze;
one hears rumors of resurrections, fantastic charisms,
but to those who are deaf, dumb, and blind,
no epiphanies ever prove genuine,
point-blank manifestations of grace are barely detectable.

In such a generic crucible
only the elements measured in can be verified as poured out,
there are no freak residues, no flare combustions;
within such an anthropocentric straitjacket
infinities, unknown differential equations, metamorphoses
are blocked out a priori;
in such a sealed universe of known stresses and tensions,
we come to expect no burning bush or still, small voice,
only routine brontosauruses and ordinary abnormalities
set within a survival-of-the-fittest bleak pessimism;
if we wrestle this time, Lord, it won't result in an unhinged thigh,
our passions will more likely boil over into dark wounds and
    irremediable offenses.

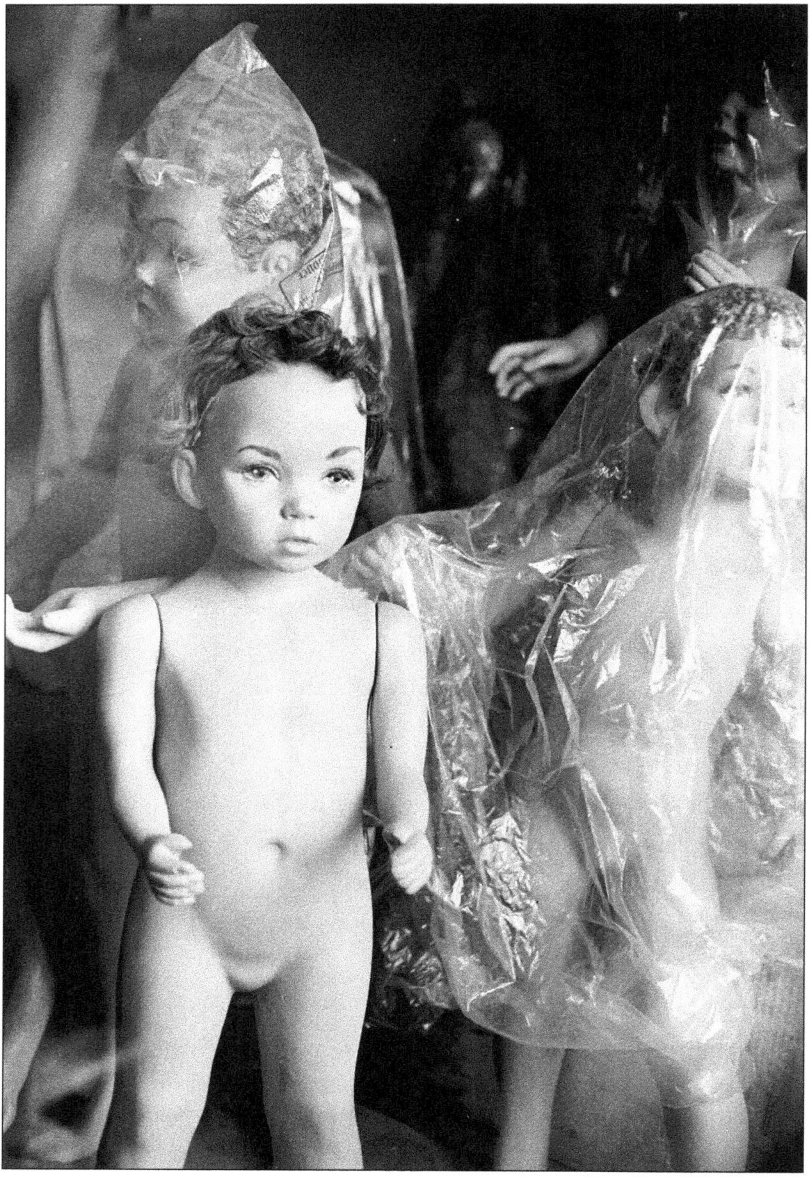

In Anguish: God, You *Schlemiel*

Mount up to God, my people,
davening, shuckling:
Slay us with all your fury
by barbarian, catastrophe, or plague.
Grant all our women miscarriages,
may our men become as eunuchs.
Cut us off before mitzvah,
squash us to revive us again.

But to what end?
Rulers forge shiny new instruments of torture,
recruit secret Gestapos, stir up pogroms,
assign us an incendiary star of David,
offer these simple alternatives: conversion or death.
Our Kafkaesque phobias are legion,
we rejuvenated psychiatry, physics,
dietary, faddish taboos.
And it's your fault.

Will you stand in the dock,
take forty lashes save one
and not stoop-shouldered complain,
wander from Marrano's exile
into a Hadrian diaspora,
never once point an accusing finger
when charged with ritual murder or excessive greed?

We atone and expiate
through the burnt offerings of our loved ones.
Pardon, if you must,
grant us thy salvation, if you're so prone,
then either annihilate this people,
or, if you persist in this cruel joke,
don't ask, "Where are faith and good works?"
we survive—it is enough,
    God, you *schlemiel*

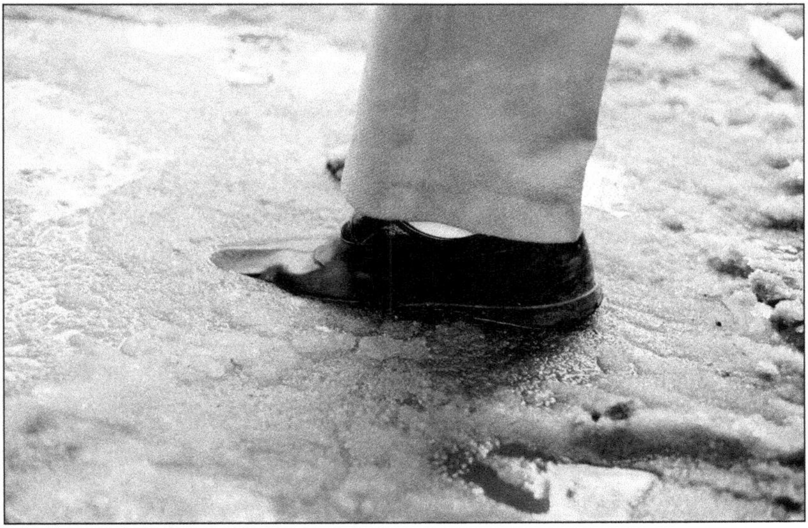

What! Is the Mocking Bird Here?

The sparrow is dead,
God, hear you my megaphone?
Teshuvah: if that bird had repented once,
the whole world would now be saved.

Here we wheeled and maneuvered our chariot souls
in the muck and traffic of sin,
once a week wiped off our Sabbath shoes,
then splashed in puddles five minutes after worship.

Some nurse broken wings, others bear diseased frames,
Hera's madness was due to Zeus's escapades,
angels rode on horseback to rescue Judah Maccabee,
Gabriel, too, ritually tore his garment.

The universe is as small as a hazelnut;
what! is the mocking bird here?
Let us regain the Center and there hold fast
or revert to Nothing and scorn the Absolute.

I lay me down in my satin box
—athwart the mighty Void—
a field mouse burrows through a broken wall,
my porcelain plumbing springs a leak.

From four-score exile we return to start,
dense as Rumi, allusive as Robert Burton,
cantaloupe ripe or volcano burst,
gurgling through our umbilical cords.

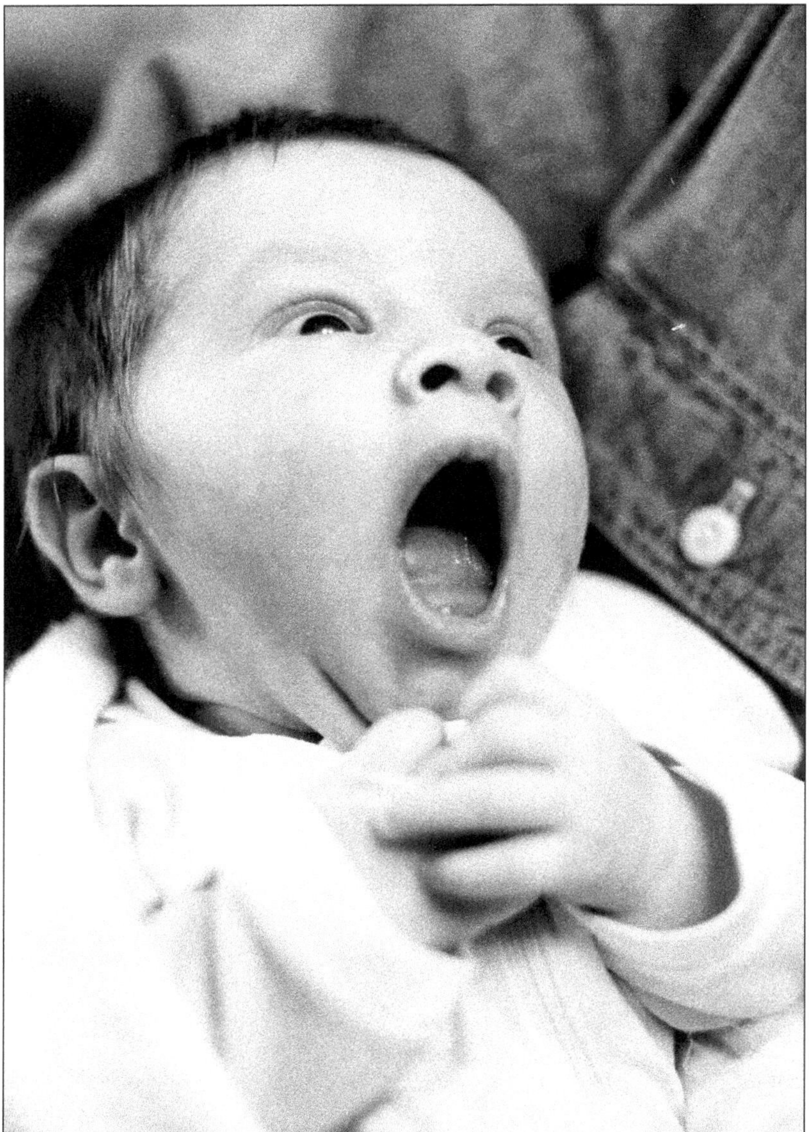

What Does God Do?

What does God do every morning
but perform caesareans,
slashing our umbilical cords,
then rinsing off the caked blood and torn placenta,
like that most astute of midwives
who fashions/forms/molds
raw kaolin into porcelain,
burps the singularly colic,
nurses the nipple-deprived,
slaps the overly-contented bottom.

Despite catastrophe and intervening years of loss,
we nurture a womb memory
of the holy dove pleading and yearning
even before we knew the power of petition,
light breaking through our weakest chinks,
the gestation period was a honeymoon
compared to the bone-jarring exit from uterus—
then we clutch our phylacteries with vehemence.

God is so extraordinarily fertile
that some feel he should undergo a hyster-vasectomy,
while all desire the sweetest honeys

rather than deep, stabbing pangs of remorse,
both are intermeshed in the warp-and-woof of this
    degenerate universe,
indeed, it would take confidence on the order of a mustard seed
for this high desert to flower into a multi-tiered, lush cornucopia.

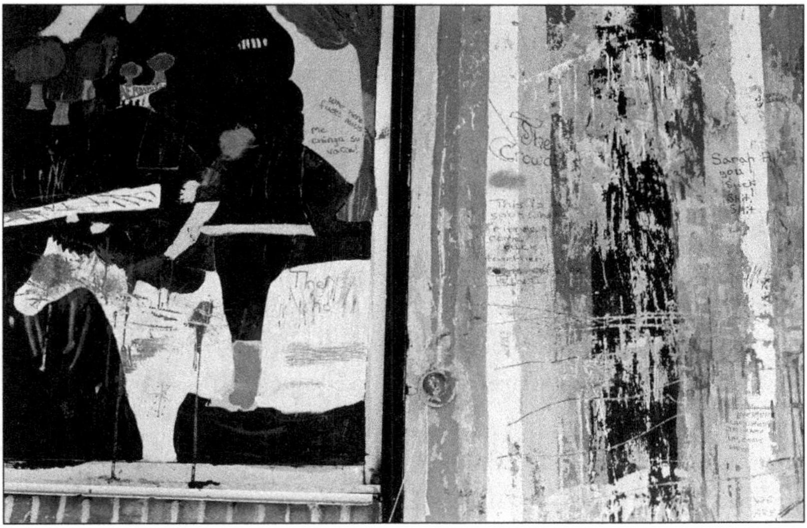

Inspired by Zechariah's Visions

The seven lamps are the seven chameleon turrets of the Lord,
the two olive trees are his two untouchable witnesses
who can turn mountain brooks into seething poison,
launch flying scrolls into robber's houses
to consume the rotting timbers,
the four bronze horns which earlier mocked and terrified Judah
will be beaten by godly smiths into self-inflicting daggers,
beheaded martyrs like those observed by Ichabod Crane
will ride on chestnut mares through myrtle glens.

A Euclidean angel will measure
the circumference of a wall-less, inviting Jerusalem,
the robes of the filthy Joshua priest will be inscribed
as a diadem with instant forgiveness,
a peaceful herb will Palladio-sprout
as all the earth waits in sackcloth and ashes
to pay homage to David's servant, the Branch,
Judah's wickedness will be set on a pedestal
in a closed basket in the Land of Shinar.

A fourth, pale-green stallion (Death)
will gallop headlong over a quarter of the globe,
the Mount of Olives be split in half,
and row upon row of bleeding palms in unison
will blurt out loud, crashing, unending hosannas.

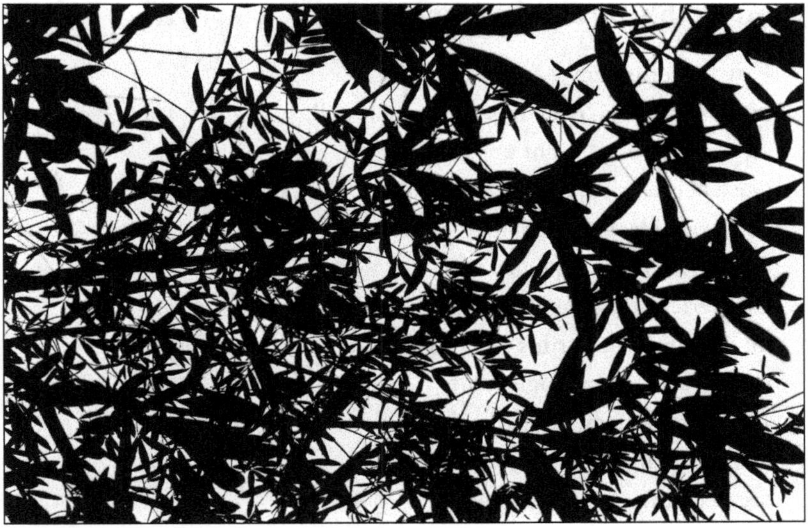

Messiah Coos and Mourns

Pray for Jerusalem
that its roots run deep like an artesian well,
its stem bound straight up
like a beech or fir,
its serrated leaves catch, then cross-reflect
the playful morning light,
its arteries prove gay thoroughfares
for wanderlust pilgrims anxious to peregrinate,
its branches spread high, aloft,
a home for sturdy, unbreakable nests,
its calyxes attract
the fiery, the contemplative.

May it fling its anthers
to a moisture-laden sirocco,
Gentiles rest beneath the shade
of its towering invincible walls,
the temple arise Zerubbabel rebuilt
—not for animal sacrifice—
but to serve as the locus
for God's regenerative self.

May the Jordan part anew,
another people walk across dry-shod,
a second ark of the covenant be installed,
Aaron's rod bud and blossom once again.

This Jebusite city, first captured by David's siegework forces,
defended by Hezekiah's shrewd aqueduct,
has been razed by megalomaniac Nebuchadnezzar,
then desecrated by an image of Zeus set up
   by Antiochus Epiphanes,
fallen beneath the Saracen's crescent-shaped boot,
looted by Pope Urban's scavenging crusaders.

Meanwhile, outside, in the centuries-old drizzle,
Messiah coos and mourns,
unwilling to take up his rightful seat
except by vox populi
when every house sports a *mezuzah*.

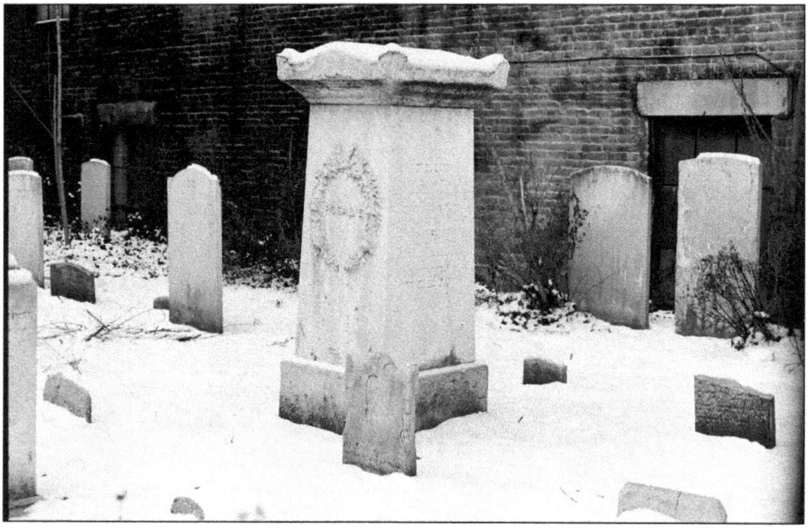

Ezekiel's Dry Bones

"The resurrection of the dead is one of the cardinal principles established by Moses our Teacher. A person who does not believe in the principle has no religion, certainly not Judaism."[3]

—Moses Maimonides

A whoosh, a clank, a rattling of the sockets,
an arcing All Soul's trajectory,
toes lock into ankles, fingers reconnect to wrists,
sinews, fat, and muscles
jostle together as in a makeshift jamboree,
a jawbone soliloquizes inside a cranium,
elbows and knees knock together
like blanched Galateas newly resuscitated,
sternum to ribs, fibula to femur,
angels root out that callous heart of stone
and replace it with one that zings,
animated carrion courses blue, then red,
the maimed and mutilated, the leprous
are baby-skin reinvigorated,
though the Valley of Hinnon smokes,
so, I say, to all you dormant, dehydrated
Hebrew fossils, arise.

---

3. "Helek: Sanhedrin," ch. 10 in Twersky, *Maimonides Reader*, 414.

Listing of Photographs

1. two girls looking in opposite directions
   [Cain and Abel: Mystery of Evil] | viii

2. trapeze artist [Faith:] | 1

3. reflection of woman walking past lamppost
   [An Addendum to Psalm 53] | 4

4. Frederick Ruckstuhl statue of "Wisdom," Appellate Division Courthouse, Manhattan [Hebrew *Hasid*] | 7

5. chimpanzee yawning [If You Don't Do Good] | 10

6. painted pumpkin and gumball machines
   [The Art of the Snare] | 12

7. sculpture of Egyptian face
   [So You Wanna Go Back to Egypt] | 14

8. mirror of urbanscape [One Metropolis Spared?] | 17

9. clock face with hands [Sodom's Hourglass] | 19

10. raptor staring out of cage [In a Prophetic Tone] | 22

11. woman looking back while walking [Contrariwise] | 25

12. woman in sun hat at parade [The Selfish Gene] | 28

13. rock ledges of falling water [Oh, for the Fleshpots of Egypt] | 31

14. sculpture of a hand [The Waterless Place] | 33

15. sheep in enclosure [The Faithless Shepherd] | 36

16. four metal figures from Syria, 1000 BC [Idolators] | 38

LISTING OF PHOTOGRAPHS

17. poster of Alexander the Great [Nonpareil: Who Can Be Compared to You?] | 41
18. male manikins [God Still Stands Indignant] | 44
19. blind accordion player [Here Come the Diminutive and Disfigured] | 46
20. close-up of horse's eye [Golem] | 49
21. herald with shield and two swords [Monarchist Pretensions] | 51
22. female manikin with sequins [Ahab to Elijah] | 54
23. man walking along wall, three part-reflection [On Bonhoeffer's Participation in the Plot against Hitler] | 57
24. incoming waves on rocks [To Tarshish I Fly] | 59
25. torn posters of female face [A Ghoulish Gift] | 61
26. man near wall looking at three other people [Fractured Dreams] | 63
27. boy with popcorn, girl turned away [SS *Mutter*] | 66
28. reflection of woman in doorway [Eden] | 68
29. closed doors on stone building [This Hermetically-Sealed Universe] | 70
30. woman playing chess [Am I Responsible?] | 72
31. woman walking down stairs [The Road Is Arduous] | 75
32. sad girl [Transitions] | 78
33. women with umbrellas near windmill [The Wind Comes] | 81
34. reflection of iron grillwork in puddle [Geometric Figures in Whimsy] | 83
35. gargoyle spouting water [Wet vs. Dry] | 86
36. two masks, one crying, one smiling [Tears: Nature's Safety Valve] | 89

LISTING OF PHOTOGRAPHS

37. Semitic bust [Exodus 28: Twelve Tribal Stones] | 92
38. reflection of man and trees in pond
    [Notes from My Nervous Breakdown] | 94
39. silhouette of a woman's face through window
    [The Wart of God] | 97
40. man laughing with two friends
    [Wagging Manikin Faces] | 100
41. man walking under metal stairway [Jacob's *Kuntz*] | 103
42. male and female marionettes [A Little
    Yiddish Humor] | 105
43. Egyptian sculpture of woman with basket on head
    [Joseph] | 108
44. funerary stele of Intef II [Yahweh vs. Horus] | 110
45. woman glowering in car [You Have Become
    My Enemy] | 112
46. manikins of children [In Anguish: God,
    You *Schlemiel*] | 114
47. foot in puddle [What! Is the Mocking Bird Here?] | 117
48. yawning baby [What Does God Do?] | 120
49. poster of rider on horse [Inspired by
    Zechariah's Visions] | 123
50. silhouette of leaves [Messiah Coos and Mourns] | 125
51. old Jewish cemetery, 21st Street near 6th Avenue, Manhattan
    [Ezekiel's Dry Bones] | 128

Bibliography

Atwan, Robert, and Laurance Wieder, eds. *Chapters into Verse*. Vol. 1, *Genesis to Malachi*. New York: Oxford University Press, 1993.
Auerbach, Erich. *Mimesis: The Representation of Reality in Western Literature*. Translated by Willard R. Trask. Princeton, NJ: Princeton University Press, 1973.
Augustine. *The City of God*. Translated by Henry Bettenson. New York: Penguin, 1984.
Babbage, Stuart Barton. *The Mark of Cain*. Grand Rapids: Eerdmans, 1966.
Baudelaire, Charles. *The Flowers of Evil: A Selection*. Edited by Marthiel and Jackson Mathews. New York: New Directions, 1955.
Cawley, A. C., ed. *Everyman and Medieval Miracle Plays*. New York: Dutton, 1959.
D'Alviella, G. "Images and Idols: General and Primitive." In *Encyclopedia of Religion and Ethics*, edited by James Hastings, 7:110–16. Edinburgh: T&T Clark, 1914.
Dean, James M. "Cain." In *A Dictionary of Biblical Tradition in English Literature*, edited by David Lyle Jeffrey, 121–22. Grand Rapids: Eerdmans, 1992.
Dostoyevsky, Fyodor. *The Brothers Karamazov*. Vol. 1. Translated by David Magarshack. Baltimore: Penguin, 1970.
Douglas, Mary. *Purity and Danger*. London: Routledge & Kegan Paul, 1979.
Endicott, Norman J., ed. *The Prose of Sir Thomas Browne*. New York: Norton, 1972.
Frankfort, Henri. *Art and Architecture of the Ancient Orient*. New York: Penguin, 1977.
Frazer, James George. *Folklore in the Old Testament*. New York: Hart, 1975.
Fustel de Coulanges, Numa Denis. *The Ancient City: A Study on the Religion, Laws, and Institutions of Greece and Rome*. Translated by Willard Small. Garden City, NY: Doubleday, 1956.
Gallagher, Joseph. *To Hell and Back with Dante: A Modern Reader's Guide to The Divine Comedy*. Liguori, MO: Triumph, 1996.
Goethe, Johann Wolfgang von. *Goethe's Faust: Prologue and Part One, Bilingual Edition*. Translated by Bayard Taylor, revised and edited by Stuart Atkins. New York: Collier, 1966.
Graves, Robert, and Raphael Patai. *Hebrew Myths: The Book of Genesis*. New York: McGraw-Hill, 1964.

BIBLIOGRAPHY

Gray, J. "Idol." In *The Interpreter's Dictionary of the Bible*, edited by George Arthur Buttrick, 673–75. Nashville: Abingdon, 1962.

———. "Idolatry." In *The Interpreter's Dictionary of the Bible*, edited by George Arthur Buttrick, 675–78. Nashville: Abingdon, 1962.

Hooke, S. H. *Middle Eastern Mythology*. New York: Penguin, 1976.

James, E. O. *Ancient Gods: The History and Diffusion of Religion in the Ancient Near East and the Eastern Mediterranean*. New York: G. P. Putnam's Sons, 1960.

Kaufmann, Yehezkel. *The Religion of Israel*. Translated and abridged by Moshe Greenberg. New York: Schocken, 1972.

Kramer, Samuel Noah. *Sumerian Mythology, Revised Edition*. Philadelphia: University of Pennsylvania Press, 1972.

Lewis, C. S. *Surprised by Joy: The Shape of My Early Life*. London: HarperCollins, 1977.

Louth, Andrew, ed. *Genesis 1–11: Ancient Christian Commentary on Scripture*. Downers Grove, IL: InterVarsity, 2001.

Malory, Sir Thomas. *King Arthur and His Knights*. Edited by Eugene Vinaver. Boston: HoughtonMifflin, 1956.

Mauss, Marcel. *A General Theory of Magic*. Translated by Robert Brain. New York: Norton, 1975.

Motyer, J. A. "Idolatry." In *The New Bible Dictionary*, edited by J. D. Douglas, 551–54. London: InterVarsity, 1970.

Rad, Gerhard von. *Genesis: A Commentary, Revised Edition*. Translated by John H. Marks. Philadelphia: Westminster, 1972.

Radcliffe-Brown, A. R. "Taboo." In *Reader in Comparative Religion: An Anthropological Approach, Third Edition*, edited by William A. Lessa and Evon Z. Vogt, 72–83. New York: Harper & Row, 1972.

Ryken, Leland, et al., eds. "Brother, Brotherhood." In *Dictionary of Biblical Imagery*, 125–27. Downers Grove, IL: InterVarsity, 1998.

Sarna, Nahum M. *Understanding Genesis*. New York: Schocken, 1976.

Smith, W. Robertson. *Kinship and Marriage in Early Arabia*. Boston: Beacon, 1903.

———. *The Religion of the Semites: The Fundamental Institutions*. New York: Schocken, 1972.

Steinbeck, John. *East of Eden*. New York: Penguin, 1992.

Stevenson, Robert Louis. *The Strange Case of Dr. Jekyll and Mr. Hyde and Other Stories*. Edited by Robert Hawkins. New York: Dell, 1966.

Tuso, Joseph F., ed. *Beowulf*. Norton Critical Edition. New York: Norton, 1975.

Twersky, Isadore, ed. *A Maimonides Reader*. West Orange, NJ: Behrman House, 1972.

Van der Leeuw, Gerardus. *Religion in Essence and Manifestation*. Vols. 1–2. Translated by J. E. Turner. New York: Harper & Row, 1963.

Whyte, Alexander. *Bible Characters*. Grand Rapids: Zondervan, 1967.

Printed in the USA
CPSIA information can be obtained
at www.ICGtesting.com
CBHW071924180424
7162CB00004B/12